Gender and Judicial Education

Judicial Education has greatly expanded in common law countries in the past 25 years. More recently it has become a core component in judicial reform programs in developing countries with gender attentiveness as an element required by donor agencies. In civil law jurisdictions judges' schools have long played a role in the formation of the career judiciary with a focus on entry to the judicial profession, in some countries judges get an intensive in-service education at judicial academies. Gender questions, however, tend to be neglected in the curricula.

These judicial education activities have generated a significant body of material and experience which it is timely to review and disseminate. Questions such as the following require answers. What is the current state of affairs? How is judicial education implemented in developed and developing countries all around the world? Who are the educators? Who is being educated? How is judicial education on gender regarded by judges? How effective are these programs?

The chapters in this book deal with these questions. They provide a multiplicity of perspectives. Seven countries are represented, of these four are civil law countries (Germany, Argentina, Japan, Bosnia and Herzegovina) and three are common law countries (Canada, Australia and Uganda).

This book was previously published as a special issue of the *International Journal of the Legal Profession*.

Ulrike Schultz is a retired Senior Academic at the FernUniversität in Hagen, Germany. She specializes in questions of gender and law, the sociology of the legal profession, didactics of teaching law, and professional communication. She has taken part in many international socio-legal projects, and conducted large empirical studies on women lawyers and judges.

T. Brettel Dawson is an Associate Professor in the Department of Law and Legal Studies, Carleton University, Ottawa, Canada. She was associated with Canada's National Judicial Institute between 1999–2016 and was its Academic Director and Director of Education. She is a past co-editor of the *Canadian Journal of Women and the Law*.

Gisela Shaw is Emeritus Professor in German Studies and has worked in philosophy, literature and legal sociology. She was awarded a personal chair at the University of the West of England, Bristol, UK, where she held the post of Director of Research for Modern Languages and European Studies.

Gender and Judicial Education

Raising gender awareness of judges

Edited by
Ulrike Schultz, T. Brettel Dawson and Gisela Shaw

Routledge
Taylor & Francis Group
LONDON AND NEW YORK

First published 2017
by Routledge

2 Park Square, Milton Park, Abingdon, Oxfordshire OX14 4RN
711 Third Avenue, New York, NY 10017

Routledge is an imprint of the Taylor & Francis Group, an informa business

First issued in paperback 2018

British Library Cataloguing in Publication Data
A catalogue record for this book is available from the British Library

ISBN: 978-1-138-69740-9 (hbk)
ISBN: 978-0-367-02971-5 (pbk)

Typeset in Plantin
by RefineCatch Limited, Bungay, Suffolk

Publisher's Note
The publisher accepts responsibility for any inconsistencies that may have arisen during the conversion of this book from journal articles to book chapters, namely the possible inclusion of journal terminology.

Contents

Citation Information

The following chapters were originally published in the *International Journal of the Legal Profession*, volume 21, issue 3 (November 2014). When citing this material, please use the original page numbering for each chapter, as follows:

Chapter 1
Judicial education on social context and gender in Canada: principles, process and lessons learned
T. Brettel Dawson
International Journal of the Legal Profession, volume 21, issue 3 (November 2014), pp. 259–280

Chapter 2
Neglect of gender questions at the vocational stage of judicial education in Uganda
Maureen Owor & Harriet D. Musoke
International Journal of the Legal Profession, volume 21, issue 3 (November 2014), pp. 281–296

Chapter 3
Introducing gender training in judicial education in Japan to support the judiciary
Kayo Minamino
International Journal of the Legal Profession, volume 21, issue 3 (November 2014), pp. 297–306

Chapter 4
Japanese judicial education: working toward gender equality in the judiciary
Chihara Watanabe
International Journal of the Legal Profession, volume 21, issue 3 (November 2014), pp. 307–318

Chapter 5
Gender stereotypes and attitudes within the judiciary of Bosnia and Herzegovina: a case for increased awareness and education
Heather Huhtanen & Majda Halilović
International Journal of the Legal Profession, volume 21, issue 3 (November 2014), pp. 319–331

Chapter 6

Gender training for the judiciary in Argentina
Beatriz Kohen
International Journal of the Legal Profession, volume 21, issue 3 (November 2014), pp. 333–344

Chapter 7

Raising gender awareness of judges – elements for judicial education in Germany
Ulrike Schultz
International Journal of the Legal Profession, volume 21, issue 3 (November 2014), pp. 345–355

The following chapters were originally published in the *International Journal of the Legal Profession*, volume 22, issue 2 (July 2015). When citing this material, please use the original page numbering for each chapter, as follows:

Chapter 8

Judicial education on 'gender awareness' in Australia
John Basten
International Journal of the Legal Profession, volume 22, issue 2 (July 2015), pp. 151–165

Chapter 9

Without fear or favour, affection or ill will: addressing gender bias in NSW judicial education
Kate Lumley
International Journal of the Legal Profession, volume 22, issue 2 (July 2015), pp. 212–225

Notes on Contributors

Ulrike Schultz is a retired Senior Academic at the FernUniversität in Hagen, Germany. She specializes in questions of gender and law, the sociology of the legal profession, didactics of teaching law, and professional communication. She has taken part in many international socio-legal projects, and conducted large empirical studies on women lawyers and judges.

T. Brettel Dawson is an Associate Professor in the Department of Law and Legal Studies, Carleton University, Ottawa, Canada. She was associated with Canada's National Judicial Institute between 1999–2016 and was its Academic Director and Director of Education. She is a past co-editor of the *Canadian Journal of Women and the Law.*

Gisela Shaw is Emeritus Professor in German Studies and has worked in philosophy, literature and legal sociology. She was awarded a personal chair at the University of the West of England, Bristol, UK, where she held the post of Director of Research for Modern Languages and European Studies.

Maureen Owor is a Teaching Fellow at Birmingham Law School, UK. Her research and teaching interests are in the development of sustainable transnational cyber laws. In this context, she has provided technical expertise to the Commonwealth Secretariat, the Council of Europe Cybercrime division. She also researches the cultural transformation of domestic and international criminal law through legal translation, particularly the interplay between law and kinship practices in pluralist societies. As part of her professional service, she has advised the Uganda Law Reform Commission on the development of sentencing guidelines for Judicial Officers.

Harriet D. Musoke is Senior Principal Lecturer at the Law Development Centre, the only post graduate institution offering legal practical skills training in Uganda. She is also a Senior Lecturer at the Islamic University in Uganda. She lectures in family law, human rights, women's rights and health law, in particular reproductive and sexual health and rights. Harriet gained her LLB from Makerere University, Uganda, LLM (with Distinction) from Georgetown University and her SJD from Emory University School of Law.

Kayo Minamino is Professor of Law at Kyoto Women's University, Japan. Her major research interests are gender and law and judicial education on gender issues.

Chihara Watanabe is Professor at Ritsumeikan University, Kyoto, Japan. Main interests are the role of the court in modern society and empirical method sociology tradition, and the flow of American Law sociology. In particular, medical malpractice litigation which is in contact with the different disciplines, questioning the role of law in modern society.

Heather Huhtanen is a Programme Manager for the DCAF Gender and Security Program in Eastern Europe. She has a Master's degree in International Development from Erasmus University, The Netherlands and a BA in Political Science and Women's Studies from the University of Oregon, USA.

Majda Halilović received her PhD in Sociology and Social Policy at the Open University and a Master's degree from Cambridge University. She specializes in research methodologies. She has worked for the Harvard Program in Refugee Trauma, Save the Children Norway and as a consultant and manager of research projects for the Open Society Foundation, UNICEF and the Open University.

Beatriz Kohen is a sociologist. Her PhD thesis was on family judges. She teaches a post graduate seminar on Women in the Legal Profession at the Law School, University of Palermo, Buenos Aires, Argentina. She has been the Head of the Law and Gender Program at the UP and has worked with NGOs working on gender justice such as the Argentine Association of Judges on human trafficking and the Gender Observatory of the Buenos Aires Judiciary where she developed a survey on gender attitudes and gender bias among members of the Buenos Aires judiciary.

John Basten is a judge of the Court of Appeal of the Supreme Court of New South Wales, Australia.

Kate Lumley is Publishing Manager at the Education Division, Judicial Commission of New South Wales, Sydney, Australia.

INTRODUCTION

Gender and judicial education

ULRIKE SCHULTZ, T. BRETTEL DAWSON & GISELA SHAW

Judicial education has greatly expanded in common law countries in the past 25 years. More recently it has become a core component in judicial reform programs in developing countries with gender attentiveness as an element required by donor agencies. In civil law jurisdictions like France, judges' schools have long played a role in the formation of the career judiciary with a focus on entry to the judicial profession and in-service education. In Germany judges get an intensive in-service education at judicial academies. Gender questions, however, tend to be neglected in the curricula.

These judicial education activities have generated a significant body of material and experience which it is timely to review and disseminate. Questions such as the following require answers. What is the current state of affairs? How is judicial education implemented in developed and developing countries all around the world? Who are the educators? Who is being educated? What are the theories of gender and equality underlying and informing these programs? How is judicial education on gender regarded by judges? How effective are these programs?

The contributions in this book deal with these questions. They provide a multiplicity of perspectives. Seven countries are represented, of these four are civil law countries (Germany, Argentina, Japan, Bosnia and Herzegovina) and three are common law countries (Australia, or, more precisely the state of New South Wales, Canada and Uganda), although the principles which have traditionally characterized civil and common law countries are blurring. The education and recruitment for the judiciary differs among civil law countries. Balkan countries have adopted principles of American procedural law and in recent years Japan as well as China have tended to look more towards U.S. American law and legal education rather than to continental Europe. Some of the countries, such as Germany, Bosnia and Herzegovina and Argentina have a high percentage of women judges at least at the lower echelons of the court systems, while in common law countries and Japan the share of women judges remains comparatively low.

The importance of dealing with judicial education and the inclusion of gender aspects became evident when Gisela Shaw and Ulrike Schultz put together the collection on *Gender and Judging* (Oxford: Hart 2013). Five of the 29 contributions in this book deal with these issues: Gender and Judicial Education in India (Ann Stewart), 523–542, Gender and Judicial Education in Japan (Kayo Minamino) 543–555, Engendering the Judiciary – Lessons from the Philippines (Atsuko Miwa) 557–569, Gender Training for the Judiciary in Cambodia (Keiko Sawa) 571–584, Do German Judges Need Gender Education? (Ulrike Schultz) 585–598.

The contributions by Minamino, Miwa and Sawa had resulted from a research project on Judicial Education in nine countries on which Kayo Minamino has also edited a book: *Comparative Research on Continuing Legal Education*. (Tokyo: Nihon Kajo Shuppan 2012, in Japanese).

For the International Socio-Legal Conference in Honolulu/Hawaii in June 2012 we had applied to the U.S. American Law and Society Association to be granted the status of an International Research Collaborative IRC, which entitled us to get funding for colleagues from B and C countries to attend the panels on judicial education. First versions of the papers by Brettel Dawson, Maureen Owor & Harriet Musoke, Kayo Minamino, Chihara Watanabe and Beatriz Kohen were presented there.

In April 2014 Kayo Minamino organized a conference at Kyoto's Women's University on Judicial Training on Gender Fairness in the Courts, which was followed by a one-day workshop on elements of gender training. The papers by Schultz and Basten resulted from these events. Kate Lumley, who is the publishing manager at the Judicial Commission of New South Wales (an organization responsible for judicial education in New South Wales/Australia like the National Judicial Institute in Canada), added a paper about her work. At an International Symposium on "The Judge is a Woman" in Brussels in November 2013 we made contact with Majda Halilović and Heather Huhtanen who have conducted research on the need for gender education in the judiciary in Bosnia and Herzegovina.

Judges in all countries represented in this collection tend to be a homogeneous group representing middle-class values. In their judgments judges define reality. In all countries it is clear that judges have deficits in real world knowledge and in skills of adapting it in the application of law.

Particularly in Japan, a very conservative country, it is deplored that judges are very removed from social engagement. Chihara Watanabe describes Japanese judicial culture as monolithic and insular. Judges claim judicial independence but are under political supervision. Also, judicial training serves to control rather than support them. Kayo Minamino stresses the need for gender training as a human rights issue which is important for quality assurance. Only in nine cases so far has the Japanese Supreme Court found laws and regulations unconstitutional because they infringe the equality clause of the constitution, although there is much more need for action.

Uganda as a postcolonial country also has a very conservative society. As Maureen Owor and Harriet Musoke describe, the black letter law legitimizes a patriarchal value system and gender hierarchies based on the subordination of women. It perpetuates the roles and stereotypes of the white male living in England at colonial times. The more exigent it is to offer gender education to judges.

Heather Huhtanen and Majda Halilović have done empirical research on the implicit bias in the application and implementation of law by legal professionals. As in the other countries legal professionals adhere to the belief that they are objective and impartial and that they simply apply the legal code. Huhtanen and Halilović have tried to map the opinions, attitudes and experiences of legal professionals and have found gendered variations in attitudes concerning the representation of women judges. They also found that gender-based stereotypes and attitudes impact the judiciary at all levels of interaction. Conscious views and prejudices as well as automatic and subconscious stereotypes and attitudes can and do affect the administration of justice.

Brettel Dawson discusses how social context judicial education was introduced in Canada and analyzes the operational principles and practices for acceptance and effectiveness that emerged in this process. Kate Lumley paints a detailed picture of the situation in New South Wales (Australia). John Basten gives his views as an Australian judge on the importance of a gender-neutral court and exemplifies where gender matters in decision-making. It shows that not only the contents of judicial education but also the methods matter, as well as the personality of the educator. Judges are best educated through a judge-led process to avoid doubts regarding legitimacy and to ensure relevance and applicability of content.

Beatrice Kohen discusses experiences with two different kinds of programs in Argentina which have been applied nationwide. In her country, a still young and endangered democracy, there is a marked gap between the passing of progressive legislation and its lack of enforcement in a tradition of women's subordination, which is engrained in the society and the legal system. Long-term impact can be expected from slower, extended programs and continuous gender trainings, as evaluations have shown.

Ulrike Schultz finally advocates integrated approaches where gender issues are an essential part of any kind of training in spite of the existence of special gender training, which in Germany tends to have the odium of ideological reeducation. She provides examples of training elements which have been successfully used.

References

Minamino, K. (2012) *Comparative Research on Continuing Legal Education* (Tokyo, Nihon Kajo Shuppan) (in Japanese).

Shaw, G. & Schultz, U. (2013) *Gender and Judging* (Oxford, Hart).

Judicial education on social context and gender in Canada: principles, process and lessons learned

T. BRETTEL DAWSON
Department of Law and Legal Studies, Carleton University, Ottawa, Canada

ABSTRACT *The term 'social context' refers to the idea that judging is grounded in the human condition and the society in which it takes place. It is probably no coincidence that 'differences and disadvantages' rooted in social context are often at the heart of what makes cases difficult or contentious. Judicial education addressing social context assists judges to respond effectively to these challenges. This paper discusses ten principles to guide social context and gender judicial education, derived from twenty years of experience at Canada's National Judicial Institute. These principles propose that judges must lead this education and should receive support and training to enhance their skills as social context educators. Non-judges also have an important role to play in ensuring that programs are credible, in-depth and comprehensive. The content of programs should be shaped around practical challenges that judges face when confronted with social context factors, and designed to reflect best practices in adult education. Local customization is beneficial as is thorough integration of social context throughout the judicial education curriculum. The value of providing social context and gender education through a judicial education organization is also considered.*

Introduction

Through my association with Canada's National Judicial Institute (NJI),[1] I have been closely involved in the development and delivery of judicial education for fifteen years with social context and gender education being an area of special focus for me.[2] Currently, as Director of Education at the NJI, I retain responsibility for overall integration of social context in judicial education in the programs offered by the NJI. In this paper, I reflect upon the lessons learned about developing and delivering judicial education seminars in the area of gender and social context. Some of these have been set out in other articles (Cairns Way & Dawson, 2009; Dawson *et al.*, 2009; Thomson & Dawson, 2009).

The term 'social context' refers to the idea that judging is grounded in the human condition and the society in which it takes place. Canada is one of the most diverse countries in the world with a continually changing social mosaic.[3] Judges encounter people whose languages, cultures, religions and contexts differ from those with which they were brought up and inherently understand. This difference may affect how judges perceive and interact with the people who come before them and their legal disputes. Beyond the context of multiculturalism in Canada, there are other enduring social conditions which shape experience and translate into particular vulnerabilities in the judicial process. The situation of child witnesses or those with intellectual disabilities comes to mind as does that of people who are illiterate or live in poverty. Systemic disadvantages of Aboriginal persons, rooted in colonial practices and arising from constructions of disability or race, also create layers of complexity in which people experience life and law differently. Gender – specifically women's experience – is one of the particularities of social context, informed as it is by histories and practices of discrimination and inequality.

It is probably no coincidence that 'differences and disadvantages' rooted in social context are often at the heart of what makes cases difficult or contentious. Being able to respond effectively requires judges to enlarge their mentality (Nedelsky, 2001, p. 103), or put another way, broaden their understanding of the breadth of human experience. This is where social context education plays a critical role. Social context education assumes that the law should respond to the needs and reasonable expectations of the community it serves (Thomas, 2005), consistent with legal provisions securing inclusion, equality and access to justice.[4] Education in this area addresses how judges manage their courtrooms, assess evidence, apply legal principles and understand the world around them. Turning their minds to the social context of the situation before them allows judges to scrutinize their reflexes and consider appropriate information to sharpen their perceptions and deepen their understanding of the questions before them.

Over the years, the NJI has generated a sustainable institutional model for social context and gender education. Our journey began with programs that introduced the experience of inequality and the principles of equality law, and provided exposure to a range of issues. Over time programs have become more skills-based, examining social context and gender within trial contexts and the judicial role more generally. The goal has been to enhance judicial skills to address social context. These programs have been developed within a judge-led organization enjoying the trust of the judiciary. The normalization of social context through consistent attention to it in judicial education programming has led to its widespread acceptance by Canadian judges. Institution-level protocols have also been put into place to systematically reinforce social context as part of how NJI does its work.[5]

This paper addresses principles of operation for social context and gender education with judges, derived from twenty years of experience in this area commencing with the Social Context Education Project (SCEP) which was in place at NJI during the period 1996–2003 and course offerings since its conclusion.[6] I am not addressing the content of the education itself in this paper but rather, the operational principles for establishing and sustaining social context and gender judicial education.

My discussion proceeds as follows. First, I will address what it is about social context and gender education that makes it a difficult area for programs with judges. I will argue that part of the cause is structural in nature, reflecting the decontextualization of law and judicial practice endemic to traditional understandings of legal principle and legal method. I will then outline NJI's approach to social context and gender education before turning to a discussion of the operating principles that can be distilled from this experience. These principles are organized around a number of pertinent questions including who should be in charge of program development, the selection and training of judges as planners and faculty members, the role of non-judges in social context and gender education, identification and focus of content in programs and the best approaches to program design. I add a number of additional observations addressing the importance of local customization, integration of social context across the judicial education curriculum and the role of judicial education organizations in offering social context and gender education to judges. I argue that principles discussed in this paper provide a sound basis for engaging and successful[7] social context and gender education with judges.

Judging, social context and judicial education

Despite the pervasive presence of social context in the judicial process, most people who have been involved in social context and gender education with judges would likely agree that education in this area has been met with trepidation or even resistance by some judges. In 1997–98, as the judicial Special Directors of SCEP prepared for the initial social context seminars with some of Canada's largest superior courts, there was an almost palpable level of anxiety about whether the programs would be well received. Participants apparently felt the same: it was not atypical in the SCEP to receive an evaluation comment along the lines of "better, much better than I expected". Even the judges seem to have been surprised and relieved when things went well. Despite the ubiquity of domestic violence cases in the courts of first instance, the involvement of highly credible program planners, and a skills-based program design, initial levels of registration were modest for programs dedicated to this area in 2010–12. The continuing reality is that not all judges see social context as integral to their cases or their decision-making process. This raises the question of what it is that makes social context and gender education 'difficult' in the judicial education portfolio and thus requiring such careful formulation of principles of operation?

Several factors may be in play here – judges may be so aligned with the judicial system and so insulated from social realities as to render the diversity and disadvantage of social context invisible to them (Harding & Hintikka, 2003). Many judges may have discomfort with, or lack of exposure to, social change in Canada. Reluctance may stem from the lingering legitimacy of backlash against equality-seeking arguments cast as political correctness. Of course, the judiciary is not a static entity: while judicial careers can be individually quite long, over a five year period, half of a court complement can change.[8] One might think that this will bring on to the bench people with a different profile. While this is true in some cases, it also seems to be the case that the private bar continues to reward traditional black letter approaches to practice and is not inherently more progressive than the bench (Kay *et al.*, 2004; Alarie *et al.*, 2013). The demographics of appointments to the bench also plays a role (Makin, 2012; Editorial, 2012; Cairns Way, 2014; Fine, 2014, Sossin & Webber, 2014). Thus, while the composition of the judiciary may be changing, it is not necessarily changing in a direction that will create more receptivity to social context as a factor in decision-making.

With that said, however, I think that unease with social context education has its roots not in individuals so much as in the system of formation of lawyers (and hence, of judges). The traditional method of legal education has tended to strip away context as being irrelevant.[9] The context of the dispute (including the people involved and their communities and the experiences which shaped the dispute and were brought into the adjudicative process), is not considered important to the distillation of legal principles through a 'scientific' analysis of law. Yet, no less a personage than Judge Richard Posner has opined that

> Law has nothing to do with science. It involves making and applying rules of conduct; the rules are based on legislative and other political decisions, common sense, societal values, judges' personal preferences, intuition, rhetoric – not logical or scientific rigor. (Collins, 2014)

Judge Posner also expressed the view that a significant shortcoming of legal education is the excessive focus in law school teaching on "legal doctrine, to the exclusion of adequate attention to facts, business practices, science and technology, psychology, judicial mentality and behavior, legal practice, and application of legal principles" (Collins, 2014). A further consequence of a decontextualizing approach to legal analysis is that context is not only considered substantively and procedurally irrelevant, but is also seen as somehow illegitimate – a factor to be resisted and excluded. While this approach fosters an aspect of the value of judicial impartiality, it is also problematic. It dehumanizes law and the fact that it is a most human institution. Thomas (2005), a retired senior appellate judge, offers a sustained critique of such legal formalism preferring the notion of a situated impartiality (Astor, 2007).

Whatever the reason, 'thinking like a lawyer' (or judge) often has not involved thinking about social context – facts in context, law in context or issues in context. As a result, legal education (certainly that undertaken by those who are judges today) did not inculcate the value of recognizing social context. Accordingly, many judges do not come to the bench with the skills of identifying and working with social context, except those incidentally arising from past client files. A similar argument has been advanced by Fedler and Olckers (2001, pp. 60–61) who argue that a necessary first step in social context education is a process of rendering social context visible.

Part of the challenge facing social context educators when working with judges, then, has been to establish the legitimacy and endemic presence of social context in judicial process. Thereafter the question arises of how judges may take context into account appropriately. The role of education at this point is to provide judges with sound legal analysis and tools such as analytical frameworks which will help judges in their work. Social context and gender judicial education has been breaking new ground, laying down foundations for more inclusive methods of judicial thinking (and action).

How the NJI responded to this imperative and the underlying challenges forms the backdrop to my discussion of best practices, distilled into principles derived from our experience.

Canadian practices and approaches to social context education

The NJI began its social context education initiative in 1996[10] after it was asked to implement a Resolution of the Canadian Judicial Council (the governing body for all federally appointed judges in Canada) supporting programming in this area (Cairns Way & Dawson, 2009) and receiving multi-year project funding from the Department of Justice. Canada's Chief Justices were determined to prepare the judiciary to respond to a changed legal world, and a changing social reality – in terms of languages, family forms, cultures, work forms and new technology.

The NJI was then a relatively small organization (ten staff) offering a small stable of courses organized around substantive law themes or orientation for new judges, using a traditional, lecture-based approach. It found itself faced with developing a new, likely contentious, area of education. In the result, it became a flagship of innovation, introducing adult teaching and learning approaches and enlivening the experience of judicial education. Through the SCEP, the NJI introduced small group learning and an emphasis on skills-building – by providing judges with the opportunity to use the information provided in typical scenarios encountered by judges. The SCEP proceeded carefully at the outset, conducting conversations with judges and building understanding of social context in the judicial process among judicial leaders. It held community consultations about social context issues. Two reports were commissioned from academics familiar with social context legal analysis and in the case of Smith, previous involvement in judicial education in the area of social context (Smith, 1996; Swinton, 1996). The NJI, through the project structure, established from an early point that the initiative was under the direction of judges and not something that would be 'done to them' or 'done for them' by outsiders. Moreover, programs would be customized to each province or court rather than being a standard curriculum. The SCEP also built a wide network of judges from across the country, who were willing to be champions of social context education and also contributors to programming.

External funding for the SCEP made it possible to hire a legal academic (on secondment to NJI) to be a National Coordinator and to secure release time from sitting for two judges who were named by the Chief Justice of Canada to be 'Special Judicial Directors'. The SCEP convened a national Advisory Group comprised of judges from all levels of court, together with academics and community members. This group actively debated how to proceed, carefully evaluated early efforts, and provided recommendations as to program development. A conscious process of reflection and adjustment became a hallmark of the SCEP.

A pattern for programs[11] evolved. A court (such as the Court of Queen's Bench for Alberta) would designate one of its forthcoming education seminars to be a 'social context seminar'. Sometimes all three courts in a province (provincial, superior trial and appeal court) would decide to offer a joint seminar. Generally, the program was scheduled at least a year ahead. The Chief Justice of the relevant court(s) appointed a committee of judges from the court(s) to act as the Education Committee for the seminar. This group tended to include most of the members of the regular court Education Committee, but other judges with a particular interest in social context issues were also assigned. The Committee was joined in its work by one or both of the SCEP Special Directors and the National Social Context Coordinator from the NJI who brought the experience of other court seminars (together with agendas, materials and lists of resource persons) and the recommended 'model' of education to the Committee.

The members of each committee, along with judges who had been chosen to act as facilitators for small group discussions and workshops, participated at a two-day judicial Faculty and Curriculum Development (FCD) program relatively early in the planning process. This FCD program had several dimensions. It addressed social context in Canada, including equality and anti-discrimination law. The program also reviewed the principles of adult education and encouraged committee members to take the risk of implementing a radically different form of education programming. At the time, small group work was an unknown approach in judicial education, with rare exceptions. This method was explained and demonstrated. Judges who were to act as judicial small group facilitators received education on the process of facilitation and an opportunity to practice running a small group with feedback. In this way, a pool of judges familiar with social context and with skills needed to ensure the success of small group sessions at seminars was created. Many of these judges continued to be involved in judicial education thereafter.[12]

Ultimately judges on each superior trial court (and several provincial courts) attended a three-day residential, in-person seminar scheduled within the regular, recurring pattern of court seminars.[13] Although participation was not mandatory, the expectation – then and now – was that all judges attend meetings of their court including education seminars. The programs tended to follow a similar pattern. There would be one or more keynote speeches given by respected judicial leaders on themes of equality, social diversity and the judicial role; more focused content in particular areas was followed by small group discussions on problems addressing social context issues. Workshops on particular topics (e.g. sentencing of Aboriginal offenders, domestic violence, cross-cultural communication) were included in the schedule of each seminar. The content and sequence of each seminar was further customized for each particular court and provincial context, under the leadership of the local Education Committee with the NJI acting as a repository of collected materials.

Phase II of the SCEP commenced in 1999. It entailed working with many of the judges who had played faculty and planning roles in the first phase of social context seminars. The purpose of these intensive FCD seminars was to provide more advanced training on social context, adult education principles and course design. Each participating judge created a module of education which was offered to their court or in an NJI national program. Some courts held follow up social context seminars. The goal was to generalize and decentralize responsibility for social context education within the judiciary, and in this way, achieve sustainable integration of social context into the judicial education landscape.

After the SCEP project concluded, the NJI made an institutional commitment to continue to offer social context education. A Social Context Education Plan was approved by the NJI Board of Governors and a Protocol for the Integration of Social Context was similarly approved. As a result, the NJI continues to offer a range of social context education. In the period 2006–09, the NJI offered four national seminars addressing Faith and Culture; Race; Gender; and Disability/HIV. An ongoing partnership was formed with the Canadian Chapter of the International Association of Women Judges in 2001. The initial seminar addressed the interaction of domestic and international law in Canadian courts. In 2015 the seventh seminar to be held through this partnership will take as its departure point the 30th anniversary of the entrenchment of the equality right in Canadian constitutional law. It will explore balances in the law under the rubric of 'Judging as Canada Changes'. Other programs integrating social context together with the analysis of relevant legal principle and judicial skills include the Aboriginal Law Seminar, seminars in the area of Managing the Domestic Violence Family or Criminal Trial, and a seminar focused on Managing Trials with Self-Represented Parties. Social context content is also integrated in many other courses – whether as a focused session (for example on sexual assault) or through informing the relevant content for inclusion in the seminar.

Operational principles for effective social context and gender judicial education

To organize the set of principles advanced in this paper, I address several core concepts and preconditions for the operationalization of social context education with judges. These were developed to guide a national strategy. However, with adaptations, they also apply to single courses and perhaps individual sessions.

Judicial leadership of social context and gender judicial education is essential

On this point, there is no doubt: judges must be in charge and must be seen to be in charge by other judges. The SCEP arose from a resolution passed by the Canadian Judicial Council in 1994 supporting development of "judicial education programs" on "social context issues" including "gender and race (aboriginal peoples, blacks, and other visible minorities)", which are "comprehensive, in-depth, and credible".[14] When NJI undertook the SCEP, a crucial first step was to appoint judicial Special Directors to lead the initiative. The two Special Directors were asked to take on this role by the Chief Justice of Canada, signaling that this initiative came from the very top of the judiciary and was considered to be both legitimate and important.

The Special Directors appointed the academic who acted as the Coordinator of the program. Together they formed a working team. An Advisory Committee comprised of judges was quickly formed and took responsibility for the initial needs assessment phase. This Advisory Committee also included non-judges.

The first program convened by the SCEP with the input of the Advisory Committee was a national needs assessment conference gathering judges from across the country and from all levels of court to discuss the initiative, identify the relevance of social context and gender education in the work of judges, and to rank priority areas for attention. Throughout the SCEP there was continual attention to ensuring that judges were involved in all aspects of program development and delivery. The vision was always for a judge-led and judge-owned approach to judicial education. Upon the conclusion of the SCEP as a separately funded project, a further resolution was passed by the Canadian Judicial Council in 2005 recognizing that "credible, in-depth and comprehensive social context education must be an ongoing part of judicial education", supporting a "three-dimensional approach" to judicial education in which "substantive content, skills development and social context awareness are continually addressed in judicial education programming and course development" and mandating the "National Judicial Institute to continue to implement social context education in its curriculum". The Chief Justice of Canada has frequently spoken in support of social context education. That seminars are developed with a judge-led judicial education organization further enhances their legitimacy and sustainability. This raises an important question about how to proceed with social context and gender education where the judicial leadership is not supportive or when an organization outside of a judicial education organization is invited to offer one or more seminars. I believe that judicial champions other than a Chief Justice can play a supportive role and that occasional seminars can be valuable. However, their impact will be far less far-reaching.

The rationale for this approach is simple: social context education done by those perceived as outsiders or as central planners removed from the experience of judges 'on the ground' will either fail altogether or be marginalized. By seeing their own colleagues involved in programs, judges will more easily accept the credibility of programming. By becoming involved in planning and delivery, judges will become ambassadors with a stake in the success of social context education.

It was very helpful as the SCEP got underway that there were judicial champions willing to take on specific responsibilities as directors, advisors and faculty members. Some of these judges had long-standing involvement in judicial education focused on equality. By virtue of the collegial approach adopted in SCEP, a community of judges was formed – to act as a resource, inspiration and network as work continued. The Faculty and Curriculum Development Programs, which were at the heart of Phase II of SCEP, played a key role in this process. The NJI was able to draw on this network for many years after the formal conclusion of SCEP. However, we realized (probably belatedly) that a process of renewal is necessary as original champions continue to move through their careers towards retirement. In response, in 2010, the NJI dedicated part of an Education Chairs seminar to social context. The original champions were invited and requested to identify and invite a newer (potential) champion from their court to attend with them. We plan to continue this process from time to time.

Three principles emerge from these propositions:

> *Principle 1: Ensure that Judges Lead Social Context and Gender Education.* Judges should lead curriculum and program development and be the primary instructors as presenters and facilitators.

> *Principle 2: Obtain the Support of Chief Justices and Chief Judges at National and Local Levels.* Chief Justices and Chief Judges must endorse social context and gender education to signal that responsiveness to social context is recognized as integral to good judging. This support might encompass formal resolutions at the national level by governing judicial bodies indicating support, and allocating resources (including time) for social context education. It might also involve speaking in support of social context education in court meetings or at education seminars. The support of other, respected, senior judges within is similarly critical.

> *Principle 3: Identify and Support Judicial Champions.* Fostering a process of social context mentoring within the judiciary will help to sustain engagement with social context education over time, and through changes in the judicial complement.

Judges who take on education roles need to be receptive to the presence of social context in judging

While the first proposition received an unequivocal answer – judges must be in charge of social context and gender education – this section considers which judges are most suited to take on education roles in the programs. Unmodified, the concept of judicial leadership can easily run into the problem of limited judicial knowledge about and potential resistance to social context themes. Social context education is often about things that many judges may not know much about and may have had little practice in thinking about. At the outset of SCEP, few judges were familiar with how to design judicial education programs appropriate to consideration of social context. This factor suggested that an effort needed to be made to ensure that planning committees were comprised of judges who were receptive to the role of social context in judging and to offer them support to learn more about their education tasks. The Chief Justice of each participating court appointed the members of social context seminar planning committees. In general, these judges were well-regarded judges on the court. Thereafter, the NJI team joined the judges' committee making available a range of resources and offering a faculty development process to enhance their skills as educators.

This process of selection and faculty development not only worked for SCEP but its wisdom became abundantly clear in later programming initiatives. In our later social context courses, which were held as national programs rather than court programs, we did not provide formal faculty development to members of planning committees or judicial facilitators. While the SCEP had provided dedicated funding for this process but there were no institutional barriers to continuing it in later initiatives. Inadvertently, we reverted to the normal planning process for courses. I think we assumed that we had a foundation of judicial knowledge and skills on which to build. We quickly felt the loss of what the SCEP process had provided. We made a serious misstep when we obtained funding for programs to address domestic violence. We rushed the process of consultation with Chief Justices on the project (due to late notice of the funding opportunity) and did not get them fully on side. Later we found ourselves working with a standing education committee of a court where at least one member was actively resistant to education on domestic violence. The old adage of it mattering who plans became abundantly clear as the project stalled. It was later recalibrated and became very successful.

> *Principle 4: Involve Judges Who Are Receptive to Social Context in Judging as Planners and Instructors.* Careful attention should be paid to which judges are selected to become members of the planning group and faculty. Planners and faculty members should be well-respected peers (judges) or acknowledged and credible non-judicial leaders. They do not need to be substantive experts of social context as they begin their work. However, they must have an openness to learn about social context and a willingness to develop a broad array of educational skills to design appropriate social context programming.

> *Principle 5: Provide Judicial Faculty Development to Judges Involved in Planning and Instruction of Social Context Programs.* Optimally, planning committees and faculty members, including facilitators, should be provided with the opportunity to develop the relevant skills as educators. These skills encompass knowledge of equality law, awareness of social context issues, and facility with the pedagogy of professional, adult learning. An effective means to do this is through faculty development session(s) at the outset of planning a program. The approaches learned in such settings can then be applied to program design.

Non-judges have an important role to play in the design and delivery of social context and gender education with judges

Although judicial education must always be led by judges, judges alone cannot develop, design, integrate and deliver effective social context education programs. Judges can benefit from relying on other experts on issues of diversity, disadvantage and difference to help them to identify social context issues in judging. These non-judicial experts need to be involved at all stages of the planning, design and delivery of courses. Recognizing this need led to the formulation of the 'Three Pillars' Principle which follows. Social context expertise is best found in well-respected community leaders (Pillar One) who have direct experience with the issues at the level of lived experience and perception. Legal academics (Pillar Two) can help to filter and translate these experiences into relevant legal concepts and issues. Their mandate to systematically review jurisprudence and scholarly research enables academics to present a synthesis and to identify patterns in judicial decision-making for review by judges who spend the majority of their time working on individual cases. Finally, judges (Pillar Three) can mould and focus these experiences and concepts into the process of judging making social context education practical and relevant to judges.

Here I must confess an area of weakness for NJI since the SCEP. Judges and academics are well-entrenched in our faculty pool, together with medical and scientific professionals. Two of the pillars, then, continue to be integral. However, recent analysis of NJI programs shows that there is very little direct community involvement, and a continuing (deep) gulf between judges and the idea of bringing community members into judicial education. This probably indicates a tension between involving the community and preserving judicial independence. Judges also have a tremendous (and appropriate) level of sensitivity with respect to learning in a safe (judge only) space. These considerations were met in the SCEP and can be addressed on an ongoing basis with further effort.

> *Principle 6: Collaboratively Engage the Three Pillars (Judges, Academics and Community Members) in Design and Delivery.* The planning and faculty complement for each course should include members from the three pillars. Engaging the judges, academics and community members in the process of design and delivery of social context education provides the best foundation for ensuring credible and relevant content and approaches in programs. Through dialogue among these three pillars, relevant, practical and priority issues can be identified and mapped onto legal, judge craft and contextual elements in judging.

Social context and gender education must focus practically on what judges do and how social context arises in their judicial roles

To be useful to learners, any form of education must respond to a learning need that they perceive (or accept) that they have – whether it be updating their knowledge, deepening their skills or examining attitudes that have an impact on their practice. Accordingly, as in all education settings, assessing the learning needs of judges is a critical first step in designing relevant and timely judicial education programming. A difficulty arises, however, when using the language of 'learning needs' with reference to judges. By definition judges are experts and decision-makers in legal matters. They are, literally, magisterial in their functions. Accordingly, judges are reluctant to state that they need to learn or that they do not already know what they need to know. However, they readily accept that judicial education – as a process of continuing education – helps them to remain current in a changing legal and social world. Judges also accept that judicial education provides an important forum for them to consider legal and social issues and the judicial role. Judicial education provides a unique setting for judges to explore ideas outside of adjudication in an adversarial legal system. This has been well put by the (now) Chief Justice of Quebec, Justice Nicole Duval-Hesler who remarked in the course of comments made to a delegation of judges visiting Canada in 2005 to learn more about the practice of judicial education, "through teaching one another, judges renew their vision over time".

The following principle, then, simply recommends a practical strategy related to appropriate language when undertaking needs assessment for social context (indeed any) judicial education. Instead of talking about needs assessment, it is more palatable to refer to 'enhancing' judicial knowledge and skills, directed to assisting judges to 'effectively manage' particular trial issues or providing a 'forum for judicial discussion'. The term 'training' should generally be avoided. Judges themselves are often the best source of information about the challenges they face given that the judicial experience is inaccessible to non-judges. When working with judges to identify 'learning needs', the task is better phrased as asking judges to identify challenges they face and the skills that would assist them to meet those challenges. Doing so makes the rationale for education evident in language that aligns with the judicial role. At the same time, this is not meant to dilute the analysis of areas where judicial education addressing social context issues is indicated. Dialogue between judges, academics and community members (the three pillars) in planning and delivery facilitates making the grounded linkages that will ensure practicality and relevance in programming.

There is an important corollary here that relates to the content of the education. Judges are not law students and they are not law professors.[15] They do not tend to be legal theorists. Judges tend to be pragmatic and practical thinkers. They want education to be similarly practical and clearly relevant to their daily work as judges. This means that information which is not directly connected to judging or within their sphere of influence needs to be filtered out of program content notwithstanding larger access to justice issues. Judicial independence must be assiduously upheld at all times. Judges are bound by constitutional, legal and ethical imperatives to achieve equality but they must retain their independence of thought and decision-making. There is no place for prescriptive education, lobbying or advocacy within judicial education on social context and gender issues.

> *Principle 7: Identify the Learning Needs for Programs from the Challenges Raised by Social Context and Gender Challenges in the Work of Judges.* Social context and gender education programs require planners to identify and include social context elements that are relevant to the work of the specific judicial audience. A broad range of sources should be reviewed including the legal and social environment, challenges identified and matters covered in previous educational programs. Seeking input specifically from the participant judges' jurisdictions is critical in order to identify and address relevant issues, priorities and resources from conceptualization through to delivery. This process should be done in consultation not only with judges, but also with researchers and community members who are affected by the work of

judges, particularly those in situations of disadvantage and those with diverse backgrounds and experiences (the three pillars).

Principle 8: Conduct Ongoing Learning Needs Assessment to Ensure Relevance and Responsiveness to Changing Social and Legal Circumstances. Equality and social context issues are so diverse, pervasive and ever-changing that continual efforts must be made to systematically seek out and identify social context education issues. Moreover, given that each person's experience of social context and gender is affected by a range of intersecting factors (Grabham, 2009; Carbado *et al.*, 2013) reference should be made to relevant empirical and theoretical literature. While judges lead in identifying their learning needs, the involvement of an Advisory Group comprised of community members, legal academics and judges (the three pillars) provides valuable assistance in ensuring that programming is credible, comprehensive and in-depth.

The most engaging learning environment for judicial education on social context and gender is skills-based, adult education. In 1996, the NJI's foray into skills-based education was limited to courses on using computers. Other seminars, including those for newly appointed judges, were dominated by lectures (given by one speaker or panels of speakers). Interaction was limited to informal conversation over breaks and meals. The SCEP faced several imperatives when it began to work with judges to design education programs. The first was to present social context education in a way that judges would accept as consistent with their independence and impartiality. Further, given the pragmatic nature of most judges, the seminars needed to be timely, relevant and practical. Finally, the nature of the area – touching upon diversity, disadvantage, inclusion and equality in the law – was new to many judges. As it was an area that touched on life experience and world views, it was a very sensitive and personal endeavor. This raised several problems to which NJI responded.

First, the subject matter could not be taught by lectures. Social context cannot be taken into a person's head, heart and practice without engagement in a transformational learning process with other judges in frank examination and discussion of experience and challenges. The methods NJI came to use (including facilitated small discussion of problems and exercises addressing specific skills) were critical to the success of the social context initiative.[16] This method is now characteristic of NJI's skills-based approach to learning: it is not enough for judges to be given information, they must also have the opportunity to use it with feedback during the education experience. Secondly, because NJI did not have the expertise in non-lecture based methods of education it reached out to others – those very few – who had thought about adult education learning in legal education. They became part of the NJI's SCEP network and led the faculty development initiatives. They introduced the NJI to adult education principles and concepts which have now become embedded in the structure of the NJI through its Senior Advisors (lawyers who are judicial education experts).

The SCEP was highly innovative for its time and context. It introduced to a general judicial audience adult learning methods for judicial education. It gathered all levels of court for consultation and programming,[17] and it included non-judges as faculty members. The process of judicial faculty development was not only required and strategic but it began to professionalize the process of judicial education development in Canada.[18] However, later enhancements to the overall education model at the NJI suggest that social context programs are now even more closely tied to the work of judges, with exercises focused on decision-making, fact-finding, sentencing and the like. The principles arising from this experience have been adjusted from their earlier formulation to reflect this later learning.

> *Principle 9: Design Courses and Learning Activities Following Skills-based, Adult Education Principles.* More than in other forms of judicial education, an 'experiential model' reflecting adult education principles in program design is particularly useful (Kolb, 1984; Kolb & Kolb, 2005; Knowles *et al.*, 2011). Through this methodology, judges are provided with the opportunity to share and apply their own judicial experience to the social context issues selected for examination. Like other adult learners, judges have a wide range of skills and experiences that are important resources in the learning process. Judicial education is most effective when it draws on learners' experience.

In practice this will mean that programs follow a model of experiential adult education design and foster a learning process which touches upon the emotional, perceptual, intellectual and behavioral capacities of judges. This entails a focus on shaping programs to address identified judicial learning needs. Program designers should craft clear learning objectives, and include appropriately sequenced, varied and interactive learning activities such as small group discussion of scenarios and small group practical exercises. Relevant knowledge must be provided, generally through short, focused lectures.[19] It will be useful to provide analytical frameworks or summaries of process steps or key principles. Providing feedback to judges is an important aspect of consolidating learning and facilitating transfer into a judge's work. Feedback can be provided by a respected expert within a small group setting or through a debriefing process (which could include comments from an expert faculty panel).[20]

> *Principle 10: Respect the Specific Attributes of Judges when Crafting Learning Activities and Learning Environments.* Judges share many of the general attributes of adult learners. They are self-directed, goal-oriented, relevancy-oriented and practical. Adult learners expect to be respected, to have their experiences taken into account and to learn in settings that are safe, sociable and constructive. As decision-makers within the law, judges will only speak freely when they are with other judges. Confidentiality is a legitimate concern for judges. Security is another concern for judges. Signage at conference venues should not indicate that a judicial gathering is taking place.

Judges also have special attributes that influence all judicial education settings, but especially social context education. Small group discussions on sensitive topics should take place in judge-only groupings, facilitated by peer judges. Where exercises are undertaken (e.g. oral communication, writing, delivery of judgment) which require the expertise of faculty members from other disciplines, particular care must be taken to establish trust between such experts and judges. Because judges are generally unaccustomed to receiving feedback on performance, particular care must be taken to ensure that feedback is constructive and appropriate to the judicial recipient's position. The press should be excluded. Faculty must agree not to blog or comment on their participation.[21]

Other observations on development and delivery of social context and gender judicial education

Explore whether programs can be customized for courts (by region and jurisdiction) and offered within the ordinary course of education for judges of the court[22]

As noted, the NJI is a national judicial education body. It offers national seminars open to all interested judges in a range of subjects each year. It also works in close partnership with courts in offering court-based education seminars. For the SCEP, it was decided that social context education programming would be best offered at the local level – of a court or all courts in a province. Given the regional diversity of Canada, court-level social context education made sense from a content point of view; it ensured that programming could be tailored to the particular jurisdiction of the participants. As a federal country with a division of powers between national and provincial legislatures, some laws apply across the country (e.g. criminal law) and some laws vary by province (e.g. family law). Within Canada, each province has a different population profile: some provinces with large cities have a diverse immigrant population and others have large (and growing) Aboriginal populations. Some provinces have smaller populations in smaller urban centers while others have larger populations and large cities.

Moreover, as the intention was for all judges to attend a program, a distributed model (at the court level) was a simple solution to questions of capacity and logistics. Indeed in 1997, the Canadian Judicial Council passed a further resolution to the effect that

> the Chief Justices commit to providing opportunities for the judges in each of their courts to attend the NJI's social context programs in at least each of the three areas of gender equity, racial equity and aboriginal justice.

Later experience at NJI suggests that the choice to offer social context education at a local court level was an effective way to reach judges. From a practical standpoint, court-level delivery ensures a constituency: even if not mandatory, the expectation of attendance brings judges to the programs. A subsequent series of social context courses offered as national seminars did not attract high registration. The programs were evaluated very highly by judges who attended, and they were exemplary from a content and design standpoint. The lower rates of registration may reflect the limited number of programs that judges can attend in any given year, with preference generally being given to those on the mainstream 'bread and butter' of judging. Lower registration raises a concern about how broadly judges will be exposed to detailed consideration of social context. A concern with a strictly 'integrated' approach is that social context issues become (again) submerged.

The NJI has not, however, withdrawn from the field of national social context programming as noted earlier. The ongoing partnership between the NJI and the Canadian Chapter of the International Association of Women Judges (CCIAWJ) generates judicial education in a wide range of areas with a 'gender lens'. This NJI–CCIAWJ initiative has been critical in developing a constituency of judges for gender attentive programming.

Integrate social context into other course offerings within the judicial education curriculum

Social context education is not an inoculation. It is not a segment of a judge's work that can be severed from other tasks and activities. Rather, social context informs all aspects of judging. Just as programs centered on social context themes should be shaped around specific aspects of the judicial role, other programs should also make efforts to integrate social context into legal principles and judicial tasks. Adeptness with social context is as much a judicial skill as legal reasoning, fact-finding, trial management or judgment writing. Indeed all of these activities take place within social context. However, such integration can only be accomplished when appropriate social context perspectives and issues are regularly sought out, identified and included in a systematic way at all stages of the planning and delivery of all judicial education. To achieve integration requires attention to organizational structure, the selection of planners and topics, the identification of learning objectives, and the process by which faculty and resources are chosen to support the program.

Where possible, work in conjunction with recognized judicial education organizations

My firm view (albeit that of an 'insider') is that a social context and gender education will be most successful and sustainable when offered by or through formal, institutional linkage with a judicial education body. Of course, that judicial education body itself should be firmly committed to social context integration. Earlier iterations of operational principles did not place a great deal of emphasis on this element. Because the SCEP received project funding distinct from the general budget of the NJI and these funds were time-limited, the SCEP was forced to adopt a decentralized model rather than a central institutional model with a focus on developing skills and commitment within individual judges, who would then be able to carry on with social context education after the project ended. There is certainly merit in building a network that can sustain itself. This plan also reflected the small scope of the NJI at the inception of SCEP in 1996. NJI had not yet assumed its central leadership role in judicial education in Canada. However the NJI changed over the life of the SCEP and in some ways because of it. By the time the special funding ended in

2003, the NJI had significantly expanded its capacity and the scope of its curriculum. It made an ongoing commitment to social context education with the support of the Canadian Judicial Council and reorganized its raft of courses and its budget to include social context education activities.

While this is a positive story of institutional responsiveness, I believe it is simply good practice to work within, or collaborate closely with, a judicial education organization rather than proceeding on an occasional and standalone basis. The judicial education organization provides formal linkages to judges, enables 'translation of judicial culture' to program designers, and involves judges directly in planning and delivery. This judicial involvement better ensures that programs are judging-focused and resonate with everyday practice, issues and challenges. The involvement of a judicial education organization also fosters institutional memory and feedback. It avoids dissipation of effort. A standalone project may make a significant difference for some judges in some locations for a period of time, but if it is not linked into broader programming, it will not be mainstreamed or sustained. At an entirely practical level, the involvement of a judicial education body with an institutional commitment to social context will provide coordination and access to funding (at least in the developed world). While the education offered by a judicial education organization may be less research intensive, less explicitly forceful and less theoretically rich or cutting edge (indeed it may be several iterations behind contemporary theory in the academy), it will nevertheless be tailored to the realities of judging and serve a long-serving constituency of judges.

Conclusion

The core purpose of this article has been to set out a body of principles derived from almost twenty years of work by the NJI in the area of social context and gender education. Various statements of these principles have been made over time and in light of experience. I believe that the principles which NJI has articulated are useful and sound.

The exercise of drafting Social Context Principles of Operation, which began in 1999, was undertaken by Justice Donna Hackett, the judicial Special Director of SCEP and me as its National Coordinator. While reflective practice had been a feature of the SCEP, it became necessary to articulate the emerging principles to position social context and gender education within a larger strategic planning initiative at the NJI undertaken by George Thomson, an incoming and ultimately transformative Executive Director of NJI. The principles were then included in the *Social Context Education Handbook* (Hackett & Dawson, 2001), a core reference material for SCEP, Phase II. Thereafter, the principles were not revisited until the opportunity provided by the commissioning of a number of essays in celebration of the NJI's 20th anniversary in 2008, including several on the social context education project. In our contribution, Justice Donna Hackett, the judicial Special Director for Phase II of the SCEP, and I crafted a revised statement of Ten Principles (Hackett & Dawson, 2009).

Reviewing these iterations again, it was striking to me how each iteration reflected the purpose and audience for which it was written. The 2001 version was addressed primarily to the judges we saw as being charged with ensuring the continuation of social context judicial education. The 2008 version seems to be a general missive to judicial educators and the NJI itself about the importance of integrating social context across the curriculum and involving the three pillars (judges, academics and community members). The audience for which this article (and its own revision of the principles) has been written includes non-judges interested in social context and gender judicial education, my own colleagues at the NJI (as part of our ongoing discussion about how to move social context education forward), and judges and others associated with education projects outside of formal judicial education organizations. In this restatement of the principles, I have focused on what I see as distinctive requirements for social context and gender judicial education. I have removed more general points about the elements of good, skills-based judicial education as these are now contained in the National Judicial Institute's *Twenty Principles of Judicial Education* (2006), approved by the NJI Board of Governors.

I believe that the principles set out in this article provide a sound basis for development and delivery of judicial education on social context and gender-related themes. They apply to those working within judicial education organizations and to judicial educators working outside them, ideally with strong affiliations or a long-standing role in judicial education. With some additional modifications, the principles are also useful for international judicial education activities. Indeed, respect for local judicial input and ownership, shared development of programming and local customization seem foundational to any international judicial partnership. The NJI's extensive experience with social context and gender education not only confirms the validity and wisdom of the principles but also the need to continually reassess them in light of experience. Engaging judges in a consideration of the interaction of social context and gender in their cases and in the law contributes to ensuring that the judicial process is responsive to the communities it serves, thereby improving the quality of justice available to all.

Acknowledgement

With special thanks to Dana Phillips for her comments and editorial suggestions.

Disclosure statement

No potential conflict of interest was reported by the author.

Notes

[1] The NJI is Canada's most important provider of judicial education, being responsible for over 90% of education available to Canadian judges. The Chief Justice of Canada chairs the Board of Governors. The NJI offers national programs and also supports court-based education in both

official languages and legal systems of Canada. In any year, there will be about seventy judicial education seminars representing over 175 days of education.

[2] I was the National Coordinator for the Social Context Education Project (SCEP), a multi-year initiative focused on developing social context education at the NJI. I worked on over twenty seminars during this period. In addition, I co-convened an international symposium on social context education in which over eighty countries participated as part of the Canada Conference of the International Association of Judicial Training in 2004. I anchored the NJI side of a partnership with the Canadian Chapter of the International Association of Women Judges which has generated five education seminars since 2001.

[3] Multiculturalism is official state policy: see *Canadian Multiculturalism Act*, RSC, 1985, c. 24 (4th Supp.).

[4] See e.g. *Canadian Charter of Rights and Freedoms*, Part I of the *Constitution Act, 1982*, being Schedule B to the *Canada Act 1982* (UK), 1982, c 11.

[5] For example, NJI evaluation forms ask judges to assess not only how much law or how many practical skills they learned but also whether they learned about social context elements in the subject areas covered. Planning Worksheets, provided to Planning Committees by NJI Senior Advisors, direct planners to consider social context at each stage of program development including needs assessment, crafting of learning objectives or outcomes, selecting content and faculty, and designing session structure and activities.

[6] My sources include the following: NJI records including formal statements of principles, policy documents, reports submitted to NJI governing bodies, resolutions authorizing programs, project reports, and program agendas and planning notes for education seminars. I have also reviewed memoranda and short essays on aspects of social context and gender education at the NJI. As a participant observer, I have also reflected on my own experience and consulted with colleagues who have been involved in aspects of this work.

[7] I will mostly refrain from asserting 'effectiveness' in the sense of correlation between social context and gender education and changed patterns of judging. Canada does not have a system of judicial performance assessment. It would likely be considered a breach of judicial independence to seek to establish correlations between education and subsequent decision-making at an individual level. Given the range of factors involved at both the individual and system levels, such correlations would be difficult to establish. I have chosen the word 'success' to capture slightly less lofty measures: has the NJI considered it appropriate to continue to integrate social context in judicial education? Have Canadian judges continued to support social context education through their registration in programs and comments in evaluations? Have the judges who lead program planning considered the inclusion of social context elements appropriate? On each of these points, the evidence is affirmative.

[8] Information on Canadian judicial appointments, retirements and resignations can be accessed through the Office of the Commissioner of Federal Judicial Affairs, available at http://www.fja.gc.ca/appointments-nominations/judges-juges-eng.html# and the Department of Justice, Canada, available at http://www.justice.gc.ca/eng/, both accessed 19 December 2014.

[9] Of course, many law schools are explicitly moving towards a more contextual model of legal education: for example, comments made by Dean Mary Ann Bobinski of the Faculty of Law at the University of British Columbia upon the opening of the new law school building, "Teaching law has moved from a brilliant person standing in front of a room lecturing to a very problem-oriented, active learning environment" as quoted in Bradshaw (2011).

[10] An earlier social context initiative had been offered by the Western Judicial Centre under the leadership of Judge Douglas Campbell, at the time a provincially appointed judge (later appointed to the Federal Court).

[11] I am using the terms program, course and seminar interchangeably throughout this article.

[12] Interestingly enough, these trained facilitators were used on an ongoing basis in most court programs thereafter. One legacy of 'the social context seminar' in courts was a continuation of the learning method innovations. One of NJI's ongoing challenges has been to find ways to train additional judicial facilitators outside of the formalized and highly concrete structure provided by the SCEP (see

Dawson, 2012). NJI has developed a model facilitator training program. The NJI also addresses small group design and facilitation in its judicial faculty development courses with judges who are involved as course directors at their courts and with NJI's national seminars. Unless small groups are carefully planned and skillfully facilitated, they will not be well received by judges (a point borne out in evaluations of programs where this has not been the case).

[13] All courts in Canada hold education seminars each year, with many offering two or more programs including regional seminars. For more information see the National Judicial Institute (2012). Public version is available at http://www.nji.ca.

[14] Decisions of the Canadian Judicial Council, other than those published on its website (www.cjc-cmc.gc.ca) are not public documents. As such, no specific citation can be provided for this or other social context resolutions or some other Council documents.

[15] As stated by Judge Richard Posner (2014), "Many academics ... who write about law don't understand judges .... The way the academic ... talks about judges ... is that they think of judges [as] being like academics [and] looking for correct answers to questions that arise in cases [in much the same way that academics tackle questions they think they can answer]. They differ only in that they are not as smart as academics. But the judges make decisions in cases that come at them randomly. So the judge's duty is to decide, even if the judge has no idea what a correct sensible decision would be in a case, or a decision congenial to the judge's views. The duty to decide is fundamental, and that makes a tremendous difference to how one thinks about problems, and what one brings to the problems ... ".

[16] Looking back at the outlines of the early social context education seminars provides an interesting snapshot of an institution in the process of change in its learning design. There was still a lot of lecturing (the role of authoritative keynote addresses by senior judges was adopted as a bridge from the familiar to the new methods. Workshops tended to be more like smaller plenary sessions on distinct topics rather than hands-on engagement with the associated judicial tasks. However, small group discussions on problems grounded in social context issues, facilitated by judges, were thorough and interactive learning sessions.

[17] When the SCEP convened a needs assessment program in 1996, this was likely the first judicial education meeting that combined judges from superior and inferior trial courts and appeal courts.

[18] Judicial faculty development is now part of the core curriculum of NJI.

[19] Accompanying notes or papers can provide extended, comprehensive analysis of an area. However, the spoken lecture should be focused on a small number of particular points that provide the information needed by judges to use in the exercise segment which follows.

[20] A rigorous process of evaluation and debriefing of courses should also be undertaken. As in other areas, ensuring that feedback is received from the perspectives of each of the three pillars helps to ensure that judicial education can continually evolve to meet ever-changing judicial needs and social context.

[21] This is an explicit term within letters of agreement with non-judicial faculty in NJI seminars.

[22] Rather than as a series of special 'social context' programs.

References

Alarie, S., Kay, F. & Adjej, J. (2013) Leaving private practice: how organizational context, time pressures, and structural inflexibilities shape departures from private law practice, *Indiana Journal of Global Legal Studies*, 20, pp. 1223–1260.

Astor, H. (2007) Mediator neutrality: making sense of theory and practice, *Social and Legal Studies*, 16, pp. 221–239.

Bradshaw, J. (2011) UBC law school gets donation worth almost $12-million, *Globe and Mail*, 13 July.

Cairns Way, R. (2014) Deliberate disregard: judicial appointments under the Harper government). Ottawa Faculty of Law Working Paper No. 2014–08. (June 19). Available at SSRN: http://ssrn.com/abstract=2456792, accessed January 29, 2015.

Cairns Way, R. & Dawson, T.B. (2009) Taking a stand: Bertha Wilson's public commitment to judicial education, in: K. Brooks (Ed) *Justice Bertha Wilson: One Woman's Difference* (Vancouver, University of British Columbia Press), pp. 278–298.

Carbado, D., Crenshaw, K., Mays, V.M. & Tomlinson, B. (2013) Intersectionality: mapping the movements of a theory, *Du Bois Review*, 10, pp. 303–312.

Collins, R. (2014) Posner on Posner: On Legal Education and Scholarship. Online Interview with Judge Posner, Concurring Opinions Blog. Available at http://www.concurringopinions.com/archives/2014/12/on-legal-education-legal-scholarship-more-questions-for-judge-posner.html, accessed December 18, 2014.

Dawson, T.B. (2012) *Judicial Education Guide to Small Group Facilitation in Judicial Education* (Ottawa, National Judicial Institute).

Dawson, T.B., Lightstone, S. & Williams, N. (Eds) (2009) *20th Anniversary Essays: A Collection* (Ottawa, National Judicial Institute). Available at http://www.nji.ca, accessed 18 December, 2014.

Editorial (2012) All-white bench is a problem, *Globe and Mail*, 30 April.

Fedler, J. & Olckers, I. (2001) *Ideological Virgins and Other Myths, Six Principles for Legal Revisioning* (Pretoria: Justice College & University of Cape Town, Law Race Gender Unit).

Fine, S. (2014) Tories chastised for lack of racial diversity in judicial appointments, *Globe and Mail*, 10 April.

Grabham, E. (2009) *Intersectionality and Beyond: Law, Power and the Politics of Location* (New York, Routledge-Cavendish).

Hackett, D. & Dawson, T.B. (2001) *Integrated Social Context Education: Program Design Handbook*, 3rd Ed. (Ottawa, National Judicial Institute).

Hackett, D. & Dawson, T.B. (2009) Sustaining social context education: phase II of the social context education project 2000-2004, in: T.B. Dawson, S. Lightstone & N. Williams (Eds) *20th Anniversary Essays: A Collection* (Ottawa: National Judicial Institute), pp. 70–74.

Harding, S. & Hintikka, M. (2003) *Discovering Reality: Feminist Perspectives on Epistemology, Metaphysics, Methodology, and Philosophy of Science*, 161 Synthese Library, 2nd Ed (Boston, Kluwer Academic Publishers).

Kay, F., Curry, P. & Masuch, C. (2004) *Diversity and Change: The Contemporary Legal Profession in Ontario* (Toronto: Law Society of Upper Canada).

Knowles, M., Holton, E. & Swanson, R. (2011) *The Adult Learner*, 7th Ed (New York, Taylor & Francis).

Kolb, A.Y. & Kolb, D. (2005) Learning styles and learning spaces: enhancing experiential learning in higher education, *Academy of Management Learning & Education*, 4(2), pp. 193–212.

Kolb, D. (1984) *Experiential Learning* (Englewood Cliffs, N.J Prentice Hall).

Makin, K. (2012) Of 100 new federally appointed judges 98 are white, Globe finds, *Globe and Mail*, 17 April.

National Judicial Institute (2006) *Twenty Principles of Judicial Education* (Ottawa, National Judicial Institute).

National Judicial Institute (2012) *Calendar of Judicial Education Courses and Resources*, 5th ed (Ottawa, National Judicial Institute).

Nedelsky, J. (2001) Judgment, diversity and relational autonomy, in: R. Beiner & J. Nedelsky (Eds) *Judgment, Imagination and Politics* (Oxford, Rowman and Littlefield), pp. 103–120.

Posner, R. (2014) Address, Empirical Legal Studies Conference, (October 23, 2014, University of Chicago Law School. Available at https://www.youtube.com/watch?v=18i5yUNJq30, accessed December 18, 2014.

Smith, L. (1996) *Statement of Needs and Objectives for Continuing Judicial Education on the Social Context of Judicial Decision-Making* (Ottawa: National Judicial Institute).

Sossin, L. & Webber, G. (2014) Judges transcend political labels, *Globe and Mail*, 19 December.

Swinton, K. (1996) *Report to the National Judicial Institute on Social Context Education for Judges* (Ottawa, National Judicial Institute).

Thomas, E.W. (2005) *The Judicial Process: Realism, Pragmatism, Practical Reasoning and Principles* (Cambridge, Cambridge University Press).

Thomson, G.M. & Dawson, T.B. (2009) Judging: social context and decision-making: views and contributions from judicial education, Paper presented at *Judicial Reasoning: Art or Science?* Canberra, February (Co-sponsored by National Judicial College of Australia and ANU Faculty of Law). Available from the author.

Legislation

Canadian Charter of Rights and Freedoms, Part I of the *Constitution Act, 1982,* being Schedule B to the *Canada Act 1982* (UK), 1982, c 11.
Canadian Multiculturalism Act, RSC, 1985, c. 24 (4th Supp).

Neglect of gender questions at the vocational stage of judicial education in Uganda

MAUREEN OWOR* & HARRIET D. MUSOKE**
*Law Reform and Publications Department, Law Development Centre, Kampala, Uganda
**Post Graduate Legal Studies Department, Law Development Centre, Kampala, Uganda

ABSTRACT *Discriminatory practices on the grounds of gender preponderate in the performance of judicial duties in Uganda. This paper examines the curricula of judicial education providers, most particularly the Law Development Centre in Uganda. Its post-graduate Diploma in Legal Practice is a prerequisite for appointment as a judicial officer. We argue that persistent omission of consideration of linkages between law and the social realities of gender contributes to ongoing gender bias and insensitivity by judicial officers. The Uganda Gender Policy as revised in 2007 obliges public institutions such as the Law Development Centre to integrate gender and equality into their programmes. We examine the institutional norms and culture which constrain inclusion of gender-related content and skills development in the curriculum. We argue that a paradigm shift in the approach to curriculum review is vital if the Law Development Centre is to put into practice the Uganda Gender Policy.*

Introduction

Situation analyses of gender and equality by the United Nations Committee on the Elimination of All Forms of Discrimination against Women, and the Uganda Justice, Law and Order Sector (JLOS) paint a gloomy picture of the justice sector in Uganda. In their Concluding Observations, the Committee expressed their concern about the insufficient knowledge among the Ugandan judiciary of the concept of gender equality and the rights of women under the Convention on the Elimination of Discrimination against Women (CEDAW) (2010, para. 13). The Committee also noted that patriarchal attitudes and deep-rooted stereotypes regarding the roles, responsibilities and identities of women and men in all spheres of life remain. Such customs and practices perpetuate discrimination as reflected in the disadvantageous and unequal status of women and girls in many areas (CEDAW, 2010, para. 19) including judicial processes and, as we shall see, the education of prospective judicial officers.

The Concluding Observations of the CEDAW Committee echoed findings from previous studies that identified pervasive gender bias among judicial officers. For example, the 2002 Criminal Justice Baseline Survey by JLOS established that cases involving women were perceived as 'family affairs' sometimes resulting in men receiving more favourable treatment by the courts. Respondents in this survey also pointed out that courts treated rape victims very badly indeed. Judicial officers and state attorneys (prosecutors) were perceived as being peremptory and dismissive in their questioning, sometimes subjecting rape complainants to unnecessary humiliation in open court (JLOS, 2002, paras 20.7 and 137). The JLOS study concluded that gender bias demonstrated by judicial officers could be attributed in part to inadequate training in how to apply legal knowledge and skills in a manner sensitive to gender-related barriers, hindering access to justice for women and girls. Identified barriers included negative cultural norms, and gender stereotypes like the assumption that men have a higher propensity to commit violent crimes than women, or blaming female victims of sexual offences for having brought it upon themselves [JLOS, 2001, para. 4.2(b) and (c)].[1]

Similar findings were expressed in the research underpinning the Uganda Gender Policy (UGP) (UGP, 2007, paras 2.6, 2.12). The evidence and observations described here support our argument that gender discriminatory practices by judicial officers are inextricably linked to the failure by the Law Development Centre (LDC) to make systematic linkages between law and procedures on the one hand, and the social reality of gender on the other in the curriculum offered to prospective judicial officers [JLOS, 2001, para. 4.2(b) and (c); UGP, 2007, para. 2.6]. This gap in the curriculum results in the moulding of judicial officers who are not able to take the social context of gender into account in their cases in an appropriate manner.

The Law Development Centre (LDC), a public institution set up by the Law Development Centre Act (2000, Chapter 132), is the sole provider of vocational legal education in Uganda. It offers the post-graduate Diploma in Legal Practice (DLP) programme. Successful completion of the DLP is a prerequisite for judicial appointment, following which the DLP graduate applies to the Chief Justice for entry of their name into the Roll of Advocates. When so entered, a judicial official (magistrate, registrar or judge) receives further training by way of induction and refresher courses at the Judicial Studies Institute (JSI), the training organ of the judiciary.

Graduates of the DLP who go on to become judicial officers are expected to dispense justice without gender discrimination. This expectation is premised on the first guiding principles of the UGP which is to achieve gender equality, and the UGP priority areas, one of which is to protect the human rights of every person (UGP, 2007, paras 3.4.1 and 5.2). Both the guiding principles and the priority areas of the UGP are premised on Article 21 of the Uganda Constitution which provides that all persons are equal before and under the law and shall enjoy equal protection of the law. Article 21(2) of the Uganda Constitution specifically proscribes discrimination on the grounds of sex (Constitution, 2000, Chapter 1).

Despite this laudable legal and policy framework, the curriculum of the DLP does not include study of the social reality of gender and the gendered division of roles between men and women in society (Gimugu, 2011, pp. 96–98). Since gender bias is a result of cultural conditioning (Schafran, 1989, note 8), the preponderance of gender discriminatory practices described above suggests a lack of awareness about the place of gender in judicial work. Cultural conditioning may also stem from what Tamale refers to as "domesticity" where African women's legal status, social standing, political participation and national membership are largely appended to that of their male relatives and they are demoted to second class citizens by society (Tamale, 2004, pp. 53–55).

We argue that given its statutory mandate as a service provider for judicial education at the vocational level, the LDC is obliged to include gender content in its curriculum and training programmes. Four interconnected reasons justify this view. First, the DLP is a prerequisite for appointment as a judicial official. Secondly, the LDC is the only body in Uganda that is accredited by law to offer the DLP. Thirdly, the UGP mandates all autonomous government institutions like the LDC, to include strategies on achieving gender equality in all their programmes aimed to address the specific gender inequalities within their sector [UGP, 2007, paras 4.0(iv) and 6.1]. Finally, under the auspices of the Department of Continuing Legal Education and Legal Aid (CLELA), the LDC is obligated to organise continuous judicial education courses for magistrates and court officials under Section 3(c) and (e) of the LDC Act.[2]

Both authors have taught courses and developed training materials that are part of the DLP. As such, this paper adopts a self-reflexive approach to explore three institutional norms that explain the paucity of gender-related content on the DLP curriculum: the narrow focus on the inherited skills-based curriculum; parochial attitudes that eschew an injection of gender theory; and a lack of cross-institutional collaboration with other judicial education providers that offer gender-inclusive skills training. Collectively, these norms perpetuate a legalist approach to the prescribed content of the DLP.

The term *gender* is adopted from the UGP and is used in this paper to refer to the social construct of roles and responsibilities in society that confers power, status, opportunities, privileges and access and control over resources on men and women differently (UGP, 2007, Glossary).[3] *Judicial official* here refers to the magistrates, judges of the High Court, registrars, and justices of the Courts of Appeal and of the Supreme Court who hear and determine cases in courts of law.

The paper is divided into the following sections. Our starting point is a consideration of the debate surrounding the approach to course content on the DLP. Next, we analyse three institutional norms that underlie the LDC's failure to integrate the study of gender into the DLP syllabus. We conclude with a brief discussion on the need for a paradigm shift in the content of the DLP vocational judicial education programme.

Teaching law in practice: a review of the literature

The course content of the DLP has been debated over many years. The debate has revolved around two arguments. First, 'black letter law' traditionalists or legalists, including many legal practitioners and judges, have argued that the LDC should provide training for legal practitioners focused on the study and practice of substantive and procedural law. By contrast, those favouring a law-in-context approach, including the JLOS, have favoured a cross-disciplinary approach to legal education in which the DLP teaches the application of law in the existing policy framework and social context.

There is a dearth of academic scrutiny of the content of the LDC's education programmes. The only academic book on legal education in Uganda is by Pamela Tibihikira-Kalyegira who focuses on the broader *policy* considerations in liberalising legal education, not the narrower subject content of the LDC curricula. Even so, Tibihikira-Kalyegira accepts the view point of the legalists who decry the falling standards of law graduates as exemplified in bad drafting, poor research and communication skills, and reduced adherence to professional ethics (Tibihikira-Kalyegira, 2010, p. 79). Such an approach to legal education focuses on transferable legal skills. This is the dominant view. It is also found in the reports of government appointed committees on the study of legal education (Gower et al., 1969, paras 59–62), on legal education, training and accreditation (Odoki et al., 1995, para. 93) and on legal education review (Sempebwa et al., 2008, paras 3.3.3 and 2.3.6). Of a similar gist are a book by the former Chief Justice of Uganda on judicial conduct (Odoki, 1990) and the *Handbook for Magistrates* which gives guidance on the substantive law and procedural aspects of judging in magistrates courts (LDC, 2004). While both books focus on the ethical duties of a judicial officer, there is no discussion of how judicial duties may be carried out in a gender-sensitive manner, such as through the creation of a gender-responsive courtroom.

The contextualists have been critical of this approach. The JLOS, a government body that deals with justice issues and brings together key government institutions (including the LDC), has identified the need to include the study of gender in legal education curricula to help achieve gender justice in the law process. The JLOS (2001) study on gender and access to justice, analysed the training and orientation of officials who are responsible for the administration and enforcement of the law. Their study found that the curriculum of legal training centres, including the Makerere Law School and the LDC, only covered 'black letter' law without any methodical linkage to the social environment of poverty and gender discrimination. In their view, such training produces legal personnel (including judicial officials) who only master the content and technical procedures of the law. The study rightly concludes that such legalist training accentuates an already gender-insensitive environment that embraces a patriarchal value system from which many of the emergent law students come. The effect is the creation of potential impediments to achieving gender equality in justice delivery. These findings reflect the failure of the legal education system to teach law in a socio-cultural context.

The landscape of the DLP curriculum review

The first comprehensive critique of the DLP curriculum was the 1995 Report of the Committee on Legal Education and Accreditation commissioned by the Uganda government and chaired by Justice Benjamin Odoki. In the main, the committee's recommendations were that the DLP curriculum should be expanded to include topics like negotiation, arbitration, conveyancing and international transactions that were in tandem with the LDC's mandate to facilitate the learning of practical legal skills (Odoki et al., 1995, para. 93). Most importantly, in considering the need for continuous judicial education for magistrates and judges, the Committee recommended inclusion in the curricula for judicial training programmes a multi-disciplinary blend of subjects including "gender sensitivity" [Odoki et al., 1995, para. 169(3)]. These recommendations were wholly endorsed by the government of Uganda (Ministry of Finance and Economic Planning Letter, 1995, p. 7). This indicates awareness at the time (ahead of the UGP) of the importance of the study of gender in judicial education.

Seven years later, in the context of a programme on the institutional strengthening of post-secondary education and training capacity sponsored by the Netherlands, a group of experts conducted a training needs survey on the LDC in 2003. In their report, published in 2007, the experts observed that the LDC had failed to develop a strategy for improving practice standards and recommended further review of the LDC curricula (Sempebwa et al., 2008, para. 1.7).

Thereafter, two things happened: first, a review of legal education by a select committee, and secondly, the development of an LDC strategic plan. The Legal Education Review Committee (Sempebwa et al., 2008) appointed by the LDC and chaired by Professor Edward Sempebwa, conducted an analysis of the core subjects offered on all LDC programmes including the DLP. In their discussion, the Sempebwa Committee observed that notwithstanding the recommendations of the Gower Committee (Gower et al., 1969) on legal education and the Odoki Committee (Odoki et al., 1995), the DLP curriculum had not been overhauled. Citing the increasingly "transactional" nature of legal work (Sempebwa et al., 2008, paras 3.3.3 and 2.3.6), the Sempebwa Committee recommended that areas reflecting dispute resolution skills like arbitration, mediation, reconciliation and counselling should be identified in the DLP curriculum with a view to developing relevant skills in clinical legal education and core subjects (Sempebwa et al., 2008, para. 4.5.3).[4] In this they gave priority to competence-based professional training covering knowledge, skills and ethical requirements. However, the Sempebwa Report did not consider interrelated policies like the UGP. The Sempebwa Committee instead took the view that it was the responsibility of university law schools to adopt an interdisciplinary approach to teaching law in its social context (Sempebwa et al., 2008, para. 2.3.7).

In the second development, the LDC developed its Strategic Plan for 2008–2013. Strategic Objective 1 was to revise the curricula, and modernise teaching methods by 2008. Although no explanation was given of the scope of the DLP curriculum review (Strategic Plan, 2008, pp. 15, 29–30), the LDC forged ahead with executing Strategic Objective 1 and hired a firm of consultants – Oak Education Consults Company – to re-examine the curriculum. The consultants began work in 2010 and submitted their report in 2011. The consultants conducted a survey among law students, lawyers and employers which reported increasing concerns about the falling standards in legal practice (Oak, 2010, para. 2.2.1). Given these findings, it is not surprising that the Oak final report focused on enhancing professional skills. Apart from social counselling in continuing legal education (Oak, 2011, p. 19), there was no mention of the inclusion of gender considerations, feminist legal theory or any other relevant subject from the humanities in their revised draft DLP curriculum.

A subsequent meeting on curriculum review attended by LDC subject and department heads, together with representatives from other legal education and policy bodies was held in July 2014.[5] Despite vigorous debate, the meeting generated recommendations reaffirming the legalist approach to practical skills training in the DLP. For example, meeting recommendations included the introduction of new compulsory subjects like Trial Advocacy, Management Skills, Legal Drafting, and Accountancy and Tax Practice. Elective subjects such as Corporate Governance, Judicial Practice, Public Legal Practice, Legal Aid/Pro-bono, and Islamic Law Practice were also recommended. Another recommendation proposed the renaming of some core subjects. Domestic Relations for instance, would become Family Law and Practice.

That a contextual and theoretical approach to vocational legal training was not integral to the DLP review should come as no surprise. The Oak Report itself cautions that any attempt to add new *content* and skills to the curriculum would require a "change of mind set" (Oak, 2010, p. 6). This statement hints at entrenched views on the part of the curriculum developers, including LDC lecturers, which would require attitudinal transformation. As we canvass in the forthcoming sections, we consider that parochial attitudes are largely responsible for the failure of the LDC to integrate 'gender sensitivity' in the DLP.

The thrust of the 1995, 2003 and 2008 reports on legal education, and subsequent curriculum reviews, has been to place greater emphasis on the acquisition of legal knowledge and practical skills to suit the transactional nature of legal practice. Only the Odoki Report in 1995 makes reference to the imperative terms of government policies like the UGP on the inclusion of gender equality in teaching programmes.

In sum, while curriculum debates have shown a dichotomy between a 'black letter' law approach and a law-in-context approach to the teaching of practical legal skills, the legalists have carried the day thus far. In our view, the normative framework of the LDC has constrained it from adopting a transformative approach to teaching of law in its social and gender context. It is to these norms that we now turn.

The primacy of practical skills – the imprint of the Gower Committee

As noted, despite the recommendation of the Odoki Committee (1995), development at the national level of the formal Uganda Gender Policy (1997) and passage of a new Constitution containing a guarantee of gender equality (2000), the LDC has failed to map a strategy to integrate gender and equality in the DLP. This failure arises from the first norm: the priority given to embedding practical legal skills in the DLP. We argue that this reflects the legacy of the Gower Committee (1969) appointed by the Uganda government to study and make recommendations concerning legal education in Uganda.[6]

Chaired by Professor Laurence Gower,[7] the Committee recommended the creation of a post-law degree centre to teach "professional skills through 'doing'" (Gower et al., 1969, para. 14).[8] The Committee recommended that this centre would be government managed and separate from the universities. The Gower Committee proposed the following practical skills for law graduates:

- Setting up a partnership
- Office organisation and maintenance of records
- Keeping accounts
- Interviewing clients and taking instructions
- Drafting legislation, court documents and legal correspondence
- Handling criminal prosecutions
- Handling civil litigation
- Art of advocacy and adjudication
- Professional ethics and etiquette for private practice and public office (Gower et al., 1969, para. 62).

This predisposition towards the acquisition of legal knowledge and the development of professional lawyering skills was deliberate. The role of this post-law degree course would be to instruct potential legal practitioners in practical skills required for the diverse aspects of legal practice (Gower et al., 1969, para. 59).[9]

The Gower Committee also proposed another core function for the LDC, namely the training of magistrates, another recommendation that was adopted by the government (Gower et al., 1969, paras 57–60). The proposed curriculum for the training of magistrates was intended to cover the ways in which a court could ascertain the binding customary rules in Uganda (Gower et al., 1969, para. 92). This recommendation acknowledged the insight during this post-independence era,[10] that the inherited legal framework from England had emasculated the native customary law, proclaimed it illegal and substituted it with common law (Paul, 1962–63, p. 190). At the time the Gower Committee sat, gender as a concept of study in legal education did not exist.

The present curriculum of the DLP is divided into core and general subjects, all of which are compulsory. The core subjects are Clinical Legal Education (non-examinable), Civil Proceedings, Commercial Transactions, Criminal Proceedings, Domestic Relations and Land Transactions. The general subjects are: Advocates Accounts, International Transactions, Legislative Drafting, Professional Conduct (comprising Art of Advocacy, Judicial Conduct and Professional Ethics, and Revenue Law and Taxation). A detailed list of practical skills taught on the DLP is found in the Post-graduate Bar Course Guide to Clerkship – Checklist for field supervisors (LDC, 2008, First Schedule of Annexure I):

Drafting pleadings	Drafting contracts, agreements, correspondence
Writing legal opinions, memoranda	Writing judgements, rulings, bills of costs, orders
Court room decorum, etiquette and ethics	Professional dress

How registries operate	Registration of cases
Perusal of court files (complete and pending)	Drafting submissions
Pre-trial, trial and appellate hearings	Examination of witnesses
Management of court, law firm, registry	Office organisation for main office and branches
Nature of firm – partnership or sole practice	Time management
Conducting research	Doing consultation and legal consultancy
Scheduling conferences	Negotiations and out-of-court settlements
Taxation and costs	Charging and recovery of fees
Lawyer–client relationship	Interviewing clients

This list aptly demonstrates the practice-oriented focus of the DLP programme that aims to facilitate a student to examine legal issues "with a practical rather than an academic mind" (LDC, 2008, para. 1.0).

This emphasis on legal practice is further evident in the DLP design where students are grouped into 'firms' (imitating a law firm) for their workshops; participate in moots [a trial simulation in which the students act as prosecutors, attorneys, witnesses, court clerks and (sometimes) judges]; and undergo an internship (clerkship) where students are attached to law firms, courts or other public and law-related private institutions with the intention that they learn advocacy and the practical aspects of lawyering. Teaching and learning materials likewise consist of case studies (or 'problem questions') that are constructed around real life court cases. Problem-based learning and moots are augmented with lectures by internal and external speakers drawn from the legal profession. Assessments include written and oral (viva voce) examinations.

The origins of this practice-oriented approach can be found in the Gower Report. As it stands, the DLP curriculum is not enriched in any way by a theoretical framework on gender-related issues, unlike the curricula at law schools like that at Makerere University (the oldest research university in Uganda) that offers a course on Gender and the Law grounded in the theory of gender, and combines a socio-legal approach with the study of law.

Take for example, the Domestic Relations course that covers equality and non-discrimination under Article 21 of Uganda's Constitution. Students discuss the judgement in *Uganda Association of Women Lawyers and others v. Attorney General* (2003). This case lays down the principle that since all persons are equal under the law, the provisions of Section 4 of the Divorce Act Cap 249 that provide different grounds for male and female petitioners seeking divorce,[11] create inequality in the grounds for divorce, inconsistent with Article 21(1), (2) and (3) of the Constitution. Students draft divorce petitions and related court papers as a compulsory part of the course referencing Article 31(1)(b) of the Constitution which provided equal rights to a man and woman at the dissolution of a marriage.

Despite this introduction to legal aspects of gender equality, the context of marriage and divorce in Uganda is not systematically studied as it relates to sensitive legal practice (or judging). Students are not asked to investigate the different experiences of divorce by men and women, and its effect on children. The content does not cover ways in which negative cultural attitudes on the part of a judicial officer may result in a case being handled in a gender insensitive manner. Students are not asked to consider how to mitigate cultural attitudes which militate against a woman seeking to divorce her husband, even where she (or their children) are suffering domestic violence or related problems. The differential impact of payment of alimony and division of property on children, women and men is not explored either. While drafting divorce petitions and similar court papers are vital to acquiring legal skills, the course fails to expose a student to ways in which their personal values on gender roles in society may influence their decision making and practice in ways that negatively impact on vulnerable women and children.

Although there is an injection of gender equality in some subjects on the DLP curriculum, we argue that this does not go far enough to include other aspects of gender like patriarchal attitudes and the effect of gender roles on lawyering and judicial conduct. A focus on practical skills need not preclude integration of gender considerations in lawyering and judging. However, traditional, acontextual understanding of skills continues to hold normative sway at the LDC. To invoke the Gower Report is seen to foreclose further discussion of the approach to be taken.

This absence of systematic and integrated treatment of gender as a subject of investigation in the DLP reflects a second institutional norm: parochial attitudes towards the teaching of the practice of law, or an inability to recognise broader paths of study.

Parochialism and the exclusion of gender questions

To achieve a practical ethos to training, all lecturers on the DLP are enrolled advocates with extensive experience in public and private legal practice. Using legal practitioners to review (and teach) the DLP syllabus arguably perpetuates the primary given to skills in the practice of law. As a self-contained system, lecturers easily adopt a parochial approach to the curriculum review that excludes any reference to matters (including policies) that fall outside the legal context within which the DLP is framed.

An example of this narrow focus on law is illustrated in the comments of a [male] colleague – K – during a 2010 workshop on curriculum review of the DLP.[12] The workshop entailed comprehensive appraisal of the DLP five core subjects (Civil Proceedings, Commercial Transactions, Criminal Proceedings, Domestic Relations and Land Transactions) with a view to modifying the subject content and identifying relevant areas for skills training. A heated debate took place on the strengths and limits of attempting to accommodate emerging cross-disciplinary topics in the DLP curriculum. At its conclusion, K commented, "The Gower Report is very comprehensive, so there is no need to change our bar course [DLP] curriculum". Although his views were not universally accepted, K's view held sway. Perhaps unsurprisingly, during the course of the three-day curriculum review workshop, introducing gender into the DLP subjects was not specifically discussed.

Review of the DLP course contents was instead closely modelled on the recommendations of the Gower Report. That all of the participants were advocates and well versed in the practice of the law, may have led to a blinkered focus on the imparting of knowledge and skills within the black letter of the law. Secondly, there may have been a failure on the part of the curriculum developers to appreciate Tamale's notion of 'domesticity' in the African context, where women's affairs are regarded as private (domestic) and male affairs are public. Tamale argues that the gendered male 'public' space is the key to power, privilege, opportunities and wealth with the result that the African woman's legal status is largely appended to that of their male relatives (Tamale, 2004, pp. 53–55). We see this 'domesticity' reflected in the deliberations on the DLP curriculum review, fixated as it was on legal doctrine and principles constructed in law as a public space. Women's experience of legal and social realities became invisible, repeating a pattern in which the public (male) construct of reality was assumed to be universally applicable.

Indeed, as Rodriguez persuasively argues, the teaching of black letter law – as if universal – perpetuates the idea of law as a means of social control and legitimises a system based on the subordination of women and gender-based hierarchies. This is because the structure and language of the legal system as well as legal interpretation are premised on the life experiences, socialisation patterns and values of males belonging to a dominant group which are then characterised as universal standards (Rodriguez, 1998–99, pp. 268–269). The curriculum of the DLP falls within this description. It is based largely on the inherited common law from England and remains largely a replica of the 1950s English common law – complete with its terminology, structure, rationale and doctrines. In effect, the Ugandan laws perpetuate the gender-based hierarchies, roles and stereotypes of the white male living in England at the time.

The focus on the acquisition of practical legal skills based on Ugandan law means that the DLP propagates a legal system based on the subjugation of women and gender-based hierarchies and reflects an insular institutional mindset about the relevance of the study of gender and society to legal work. Therefore it is not surprising that the DLP content has remained largely unchanged since the LDC's inception in 1970.

This parochial norm could be disrupted by engaging in dialogue and collaboration with other institutions which adopt other modes of thought about how to integrate gender theory into practice-oriented course content. These institutions could include other judicial education bodies or organisations in other sectors that nevertheless interact with the legal sector. From such dialogue could come proficiency in integrating the experiences of women and children in a practical manner. In our view, however, a third norm – resistance to cross-institutional collaboration – is in play.

Lack of cross-institutional collaboration in judicial education

Previous government reports, like the Odoki Report, have underscored the need for the LDC, the judiciary and the Ministry of Justice to collaborate in organising continuous judicial education addressing gender and informed by associated gender theory (Odoki et al., 1995, paras 37–38). As noted, there is little evidence that the LDC has acted on these reports. We suggest that due to its dominant status as a sole provider of vocational legal training, the LDC has not *needed* to partner with either national providers of continuing judicial education, or regional and international judicial training institutes despite its lack of expertise on how to integrate theory into a practical course.

There is no lack of institutions that offer legal education and upon which judicial education could draw. At the post-DLP qualification stage, the Judicial Studies Institute of Uganda (JSI) (JSI website, 2014) has, since its inception in 2004, provided continuing judicial education to judges through in-house training of judicial officers during their induction and refresher courses across their career. The JSI has included topics such as Gender in the Social Context, using learning materials which include the JLOS *Gender and Access to Justice Study* Report. The National Association of Women Judges-Uganda [NAWJ(U)] has offered judicial seminars open to all judges on the jurisprudence of equality (Wolayo, 2007). The Ministry of Gender, Labour and Social Development has developed programmes on the UGP, preparing gender training materials and becoming involved in training judicial officers in gender and access to justice [JLOS, 2001, para. 3.1.6(a)]. At the regional level is the East African Judicial Education Committee, a subsidiary body of the sectoral Council on Legal and Judicial Affairs of the East African Community, which aims to harmonise legal training, certification, practice framework and curriculum within the East African countries.

Guidance could also be sought at the international level from the UN Women, the United Nations *Entity for Gender Equality and the Empowerment of Women* (2012) which offers a wide range of training services in gender-related areas.

Other judicial education organisations are a natural resource for the LDC. The Judicial College of England and Wales (JC) has a well-developed curriculum of training available to judges and tribunal members and a strategic commitment to international training activities (Strategy of the Judicial College, 2015–2017). The JC maintains an *Equal Treatment Bench Book* (Judicial College, 2013) which addresses dimensions of gender equality in including the meaning of gender stereotyping, and the social context in which victims (especially women) live. These diverse topics are intended to help a judicial official realise gender equality in the court room. Given Commonwealth linkages and shared common law principles, resources available through the JC should be relevant to the training offered in the DLP.

There is little indication that the LDC has collaborated with related or cross-disciplinary institutions with a view to integrating gender in its curriculum. This may be due in part to the LDC's status as an independent statutory vocational service provider. As such, the LDC operates in an autonomous manner with its training content largely decided upon by its lecturers with some external input from members of the legal profession who sit on the Bar Course Advisory Board.

Another resource in thinking about legal education is the university sector. The School of Law at Makerere University – the oldest research university in Uganda – offers, as mentioned, a course on Gender and the Law that is socio-legal in orientation. Research and practice within university law programmes are guided by theoretical approaches within law and from other disciplines like sociology that help to make sense of why things happen in a certain way thereby informing responses to social and legal problems. Of direct relevance to judicial reasoning and decision-making are feminist judgement projects such as the feminist judgements project at the York Law School at the University of York in England. Through this project, law students are introduced to the gendered nature of law decision making and asked to consider whether there is a female voice in judging (Hunter & Fitzpatrick, 2012, pp. 261–265). In so doing, the project draws on Rosemary Hunter's theory of feminist judgements which highlights the importance of challenging gender bias; contextualising and particularising; promoting substantive equality; and drawing on feminist scholarship (Hunter, 2008, pp. 10–15). Rosemary Hunter also maintains that judges can consider the different experiences of men and women, yet remain independent and impartial (Hunter, 2008, pp. 10–15, 18–30). Such an interdisciplinary approach allows students to explore the diverse ways in which 'extrinsic' factors, like gender stereotypes, influence the execution of judicial duties. Using an infusion of transactional skills *and* gender-based feminist theory offers a legal practitioner or judicial officer a richer set of skills through which to avoid gender bias.

Given the likely inability of the LDC to itself become a research intensive institution (Kashaka, 2014), collaboration with law faculties from universities which are part of the African Association of Universities (AAU, 2012) seems particularly promising. In this regard, a joint workshop – the first of its kind – was held between Ugandan law schools and the LDC on 23rd November 2010. Participants resolved to hold an annual event to consider the alignment of law school curricula and the LDC through consideration of topics covered in the undergraduate law degree programmes of each university and those covered in the DLP programme and constructive critique of each institution's curriculum. Such a commendable initiative, if carried forward, suggests that it may be possible to shift this third normative barrier to opening of the DLP curriculum and inclusion of theoretically rich content into the vocational stage of judicial education.

Concluding reflections

The DLP curriculum currently lacks an appropriate connection between law and its technical procedures, and gender issues. Continuing gender discriminatory practices by judicial officers, all of whom are graduates of the DLP programme, indicate a clear need for change. We have discussed several normative factors that have exacerbated the absence of gender-related theory in the curriculum. First is a sharp tilt towards greater practical skills training to accommodate the professional standards of the legal practice. Second, has been an enduring parochial approach to curriculum review which has failed to transcend the existing paradigms of DLP curriculum. Thirdly, a lack of cross-institutional collaboration with other legal and judicial education providers has shut off the LDC from comparative practices of gender-responsive lawyering and judging.

We suggest that the LDC should look further afield to draw on experiences of how to integrate gender into the curriculum. In this respect, proposals by Vain (1998–1999, p. 264) are instructive. Vain suggests that the first challenge to introducing gender-based studies into legal education is an explicit recognition of the lack of gender issues in the curriculum. The next step is for the lecturers and students to educate themselves about the area. Accordingly, an important step for the LDC as an autonomous statutory government institution would be to start with an acknowledgment of their current lack of gender theory in the curriculum and create opportunities for the teaching staff to attend awareness training on gender. Thereafter, the LDC should explore ways in which it could implement the UGP in its training programmes. In this work, Module 4 on mainstreaming gender in the curriculum prepared by the AAU provides a relevant resource as it outlines relevant topics such as defining reality, exploring sex roles and stereotypes and the steps to be taken to achieve integrated gender knowledge across the curriculum. Following this process at an institutional and programmatic level should assist the LDC in implementing the recommendations of CEDAW (CEDAW, 2010, paras 14 and 24) in favour of providing gender-sensitive training for prospective judicial officers.

Other innovative initiatives could be undertaken that would strengthen both the professional skills of participants in the DLP and their contextual awareness and responsiveness. A successful experiment in 2011 in which a Criminal Proceedings team worked in partnership with the judiciary to create a novel approach to vocational training, offers a model in this regard.[13] In this innovation, the newly established Magistrates' Court at the LDC held a court session at the main auditorium on the LDC campus in October 2011 at which actual court proceedings were observed by 400 plus DLP students. The Court sat during the first term when the students were covering trial procedures in magistrates' courts. DLP students were able to see and hear 'live' cases and, most importantly, to engage in an interactive question–answer session with the presiding magistrate at the close of the Court session. This interaction allowed DLP students to appreciate the workings of the Court and the context of the cases before it. It would provide an ideal venue for modelling the operation of a gender-responsive court. Furthermore, with the introduction by the JSI of gender and equality studies in their syllabus, the idea of Court sittings at the LDC campus could be replicated by the superior courts including the High Court, Court of Appeal and even the Supreme Court. Through holding court sessions on the LDC campus, the LDC could investigate ways in which it can collaborate with the JSI to train prospective (or serving) judicial officials to be better able to dispense justice in a gender-responsive manner.

While we conclude our discussion on this optimistic note, we recognise that our analysis of LDC and the curriculum in the DLP indicates the need for a paradigm shift in the approach to curriculum design. Entrenched norms will need to be opened to scrutiny and the possibility of change. The path forward may be through adopting and adapting some of the techniques and practices of creating a gender-responsive learning environment as discussed in this paper. Properly implemented, such a move ought to facilitate a better understanding of the place of gender and equality in judicial work.

Acknowledgements

The authors thank the members of Panel 02 on Gender and Judicial Education (Hawaii), the Governance, Regulation and Family Law research unit at the University of Bristol Law School, and the journal reviewers for their constructive comments.

Disclosure statement

No potential conflict of interest was reported by the authors.

Notes

[1] Other areas of gender inequality include the denial of women's rights to land (women only have user rights), the violation of a woman's right to choose whether to marry at 18 (girls below that age are sometimes forced into marriage) and the prevalence of gender-based violence against women and girls including acts of domestic violence, rape and defilement (UGP, 2007, paras 2.7, 2.8 and 2.10). For other academic works on diverse aspects of gender inequality in Uganda see: Tibatemwa-Ekirikubinza (1998) on multiple partnering, gender relations and violence by women; Tuhaise (2000–2001) on gender and property relations; and Musoke (2002–2003) on female genital mutilation and the clash between culture and human rights.

[2] Although since 2000 the LDC had not offered continuing judicial education courses partly due to the gradual phasing out of the lay magistracy for whom the programme was intended.

[3] The authors acknowledge Gimugu's observation about the inflexible gender order that is intolerant to gender diversity and regards a person as either male or female (2011, 100), and the wealth of literature on sexual orientation bias in the judiciary at the international level – see for instance Bridgewater and Smith (2002). Still, this paper discusses gender only in the context of the UGP (2007).

[4] For a detailed discussion of developments in legal education in Uganda, see Tibihikira-Kalyegira (2010).

[5] The meeting was held on 1 July 2014 at the LDC. Participants included LDC subject and departmental heads, the chair of the Committee on Continuing Legal Education of the Uganda Law Council, deans of law schools that offer the qualifying law degree, and representatives from the Ministry of Justice and Constitutional Affairs, the Uganda Law Reform Commission and JLOS. The Management Committee, which is the policy-making body of LDC, has not yet adopted the Oak Report, draft curriculum or any related recommendations (at time of going to press).

[6] As Allott reminds us, Britain was often looked to as having a special responsibility to develop legal education in its former colonies because their legal systems and common law principles were derived from those of England (Allott, 1960, p. 132). Subjugation of women and reinforcement of gender hierarchies was another aspect of the inherited legal system and its accompanying legal education.

[7] Professor Laurence Gower had been the Cassel Professor of Commercial Law in London University and, between 1962 and 1965, he had worked as an adviser to the Nigerian Council and as Dean and Professor of Law at the University of Lagos [see Obituary (1998)].

[8] A summary of the government's proposals are provided in *Journal of African Law* (Anon, 1970, 2–4).

[9] This recommendation was adopted by the government (Gower et al., 1969, paras 32, 33 and 34).

[10] Uganda became an independent state on 9 October 1962.

[11] Under Section 4 of the Divorce Act, a male petitioner can only cite one ground (adultery) for divorce, while a female petitioner has more options.

[12] Curriculum Review training (4–7 June 2010, Colline Hotel, Mukono Uganda). Both authors participated in this training.

[13] Maureen Owor (one of the authors) was part of the team that hosted the court session at the LDC campus.

References

African Association of Universities. (2012) *Mainstreaming Gender in the Curriculum*, available at: http://www2.aau.org/wghe/gender/toolkit/Toolkit-module4.pdf). Last accessed on 12th December 2012.

Allott, A.N. (1960) Legal education in East Africa, *Journal of African Law*, 4, pp. 130–132.
Anon. (1970) The future of legal education in Uganda: reviewed work(s), *Journal of African Law*, 14(1), pp. 1–4.
Bridgewater, D.P. & Smith, V.B. (2002) Homophobia in the halls of justice: sexual orientation bias and its implications within the legal system, *Journal of Gender, Social Policy and the Law*, 11(1), pp. 1–8.
Concluding Observations, Committee on the Elimination of Discrimination against Women. (22nd October 2010) CEDAW/C/UGA/CO/7.
Constitution of the Republic of Uganda, Chapter 1 (Laws of Uganda 2000).
Gimugu, K. (2011) Gender: getting to grips with sex and gender pluralism, *Journal of Uganda Judicial Officers Association*, 17, pp. 96–103.
Gower, L.C.B. Johnstone, Q. & Stevens, R.B. (1969) Government Memorandum on a Report of a Committee Appointed to Study and Make Recommendations Concerning Legal Education in Uganda, Session Paper 3 of 1969.
Hunter, R. (2008) Can feminist judges make a difference? *International Journal of the Legal Profession*, 15(1–2), pp. 7–36.
Hunter, C. & Fitzpatrick, B. (2012) Feminist judging and legal theory, *The Law Teacher*, 46(3), pp. 255–267.
Judicial College. (2013) Equal Treatment Bench Book. Judicial College. Available at http://www.judiciary.gov.uk/publications/equal-treatment-bench-book/, accessed 28th September 2014.
Judicial Studies Institute of Uganda, General Information. Available at: http://www.jsi-uganda.org/index.php/learning-material/effectiveness, accessed on 9th September 2014.
Justice, Law and Order Sector. (2001) *Gender and Access to Justice* (Kampala, Justice, Law and Order Sector).
Justice, Law and Order Sector. (2002) *Criminal Justice Baseline Survey* (Kampala, Justice, Law and Order Sector).
Kashaka, U. (2014) LDC needs sh5b for construction, *New Vision* 23rd April.
Law Development Centre Act, Chapter 132 (Laws of Uganda 2000).
Law Development Centre. (2004) *A Handbook for Magistrates* (Kampala, Law Development Centre Publishers).
Law Development Centre. (2008) Report of the Committee on Clerkship Guidelines for Law Development Centre (LDC) Courses (Kampala, Law Development Centre).
Law Development Centre. (2008) Strategic Plan for 2008–2013 (Kampala, Law Development Centre).
Minister of Finance and Economic Planning Letter to the World Bank 20th December 1995.
Musoke, H. D. (2002–2003). The clash between culture and human rights: a case of female genital mutilation, *The Uganda Law Focus*, pp. 1–19.
Oak Education Consults Company Ltd. (September 2010) *Curriculum Needs Assessment Report* (Kampala, Oak Education Consults Company Ltd).
Oak Education Consults Company Ltd. (March 2011) *Detailed Description of the Bar Programme* (Kampala, Oak Education Consults Company Ltd).
Obituary Professor Laurence Gower. (1998) The Independent, 12 February 1998. Available at http://www.independent.co.uk/news/obituaries/obituary-professor-laurence-gower-1144314.html, accessed September 9, 2014.
Odoki, B.J. (1990) *An Introduction to Judicial Conduct and Practice*. 3rd ed (Kampala, LDC Publishers).
Odoki, B.J. Asante, K.B. Jjuuko, F.W. & Bossa, S.B. (September 1995) *Final Report of the Committee on Legal Education, Training and Accreditation in Uganda* (Kampala, Government of Uganda).
Paul, C.N.J. (1962–1963) Legal education in English-speaking Africa, *Journal of Legal Education*, 15, pp. 189–204.
Rodriguez, V.M. (1998–1999) Pedagogy and law: ideas for integrating gender into legal education, *Journal of Gender, Social Policy and the Law*, 7, pp. 267–278.
Schafran, H.L. (1989) Gender bias in the courts: an emerging focus for judicial reform, *Arizona State Law Journal*, 21, pp. 287–274.
Sempebwa, E., Wandira, A. Hol, T. & Nakachwa, F. (2008) *Final Report on the Legal Education Review in Uganda* (Kampala, Law Development Centre).

Strategy of the Judicial College 2015–2017. (2015) Judicial College, available at http://www.judiciary.gov.uk/publications/judicial-college-strategy-2015-2017, accessed January 31, 2015.

Tamale, S. (2004) Gender trauma in Africa: enhancing women's links to resources, *Journal of African Law*, 48(1), pp. 50–61.

Tibatemwa-Ekirikubinza, L. (1998) Multiple partnering, gender relations and violence by women: reflections from Uganda's penal regime, *East African Journal of Peace and Human Rights*, 4(1), pp. 15–40.

Tibihikira-Kalyegira, P. (2010) *Liberalisation of Legal Education in Uganda: Policy Considerations* (Kampala, LawAfrica Publishers).

Tuhaise, P. (2000/2001) Gender and property relations in Uganda, *The Uganda Law Focus*, 1(1), pp. 53–71.

Uganda Association of Women Lawyers v. Attorney General Constitutional Petition 2 of 2003, [2004] UGCC 1.

Uganda Gender Policy 1997 (revised in 2007), Ministry of Gender, Labour and Community Development.

United Nations Women. (2012) United Nations Entity for Gender Equality and the Empowerment of Women, Available at http://www.unwomen.org/en, accessed on 9 September 2014.

Vain, L. (1998–1999) Integrating gender into legal education: obstacles and challenges, *Journal of Gender, Social Policy and the Law*, 7, pp. 261–266.

Wolayo, H. (2007) Role of Women Judges Associations: A Perspective from Uganda. *Newsletter of the International Association of Women Judges*, November.

Introducing gender training in judicial education in Japan to support the judiciary

KAYO MINAMINO
Faculty for the Study of Contemporary Society, Kyoto Women's University, Kyoto, Japan

ABSTRACT *In this paper, I will present the necessity of introducing gender training in continuing legal education, especially judicial education. Gender-related topics are rarely covered by professional legal education in Japan, and no systematic effort has been made to address gender in continuing education. In view of the current situation, I will explain the necessity of continuing legal education as well as the necessity of including gender training in judicial education by clarifying the principles of the judicial education systems implemented overseas and the values underlying these systems, while taking into account the role of the judiciary in the development of the law. I will show that these values and the use of support-based judicial education as a means of achieving them should be acceptable for the Japanese judiciary as well. At the same time, I will urge a shift in judicial philosophy from the current model of maintaining the judiciary's independence, which leaves it insular and homogenous, to a new model: a judiciary which is accessible and supported by the confidence of the public.*

Gender education in professional legal education in Japan

In Japan, the first stage of legal education is the undergraduate law faculties of universities. At this stage, students receive a broad education in law and learn how to view issues from a legal perspective. The current professional legal qualification system makes law schools responsible for providing educational courses to develop legal professionals.

Gender education in professional legal education

Law school curricula are focused on qualifying students to take the bar examination. Completion of undergraduate courses in law is not a requirement for taking law school entrance examinations. After completing law school education and passing the bar examination, students receive practical training at the Supreme Court-affiliated Legal Training and Research Institute (hereinafter the 'Institute'). Upon completing training and passing a final examination, they begin careers as legal professionals. At this point, new legal professionals choose one of the three career paths: judge, public prosecutor or attorney. Very few particularly prestigious national law schools include classes specialized in gender issues in their curricula. On the other hand, some private law schools which admit elite students provide several gender classes. All in all, gender is not considered to be an obligatory or priority subject in professional legal education[1] (Science Council of Japan Gender Law Committee, 2014).

Gender education in continuing legal education

On-the-job training in each of the three practical fields of law has been considered to play the most important role in continuing legal education (CLE). The Institute is responsible for judges' CLE, while the Ministry of Justice and bar associations provide training programs for public prosecutors and attorneys, respectively. According to Watanabe (2015), the Institute does not provide any independent training program on the subject of gender. Gender is addressed only as a human rights education topic. Furthermore, there is a view with regard to judicial CLE (judicial education) in Japan that consultative meetings of judges organized by the respective divisions of the Supreme Court Secretariat have a greater influence on the substantive outcomes of litigation than training programs provided by the Institute (Miyazawa & Kisa, 2009). In fact, in a series of cases involving employment discrimination against women that arose around the end of the twentieth century, including the Sumitomo Denki Kyogyo case,[2] the conclusion presented by the Supreme Court Secretariat at the consultative meetings held among judges hearing similar cases presumably influenced the judgments (Minamino, 2013). Thus, the legal stability (consistency of judicial outcomes) (Sato, 2000) to which the Supreme Court of Japan attaches such importance could be perceived by an objective observer to be inconsistent with the fundamental rule of judicial independence.

In the section below, I will review the general meaning and necessity of CLE and the objectives and methods of judicial education, and discuss the necessity of including gender training in CLE.

Continuing legal education objectives

Generally, CLE has the direct objective of improving legal services by improving the capabilities of legal professionals, thereby assuring service quality and gaining public confidence in legal professionals.

Providers of legal services and human rights

People seek legal services to vindicate their rights. Because of this, a failure to ensure the quality of legal services would not only violate people's human rights or other rights but would also undermine their confidence in the legal system as a whole. Legal professionals will be unable to win the public's confidence if legal service quality is unreliable. Public opinion regarding the legal system could also change depending on the level of public confidence in the fairness of the system.

Because legal services are provided directly to users in individual cases, a person's confidence in the legal professionals with whom he/she directly communicates is closely related to his/her confidence in the legal system as a whole. The judicial branch will be unable to fulfill its functions unless legal professionals are trusted to be fair, and people understand the fairness of legal professionals to represent the fairness of the overall legal system. People who lack confidence in legal professionals would be unlikely to choose the judicial process as a means of resolving their disputes. Disputants would be left with no choice but to resort to extra-judicial means. This could result in disputes being settled in a manner that is unacceptable from the perspective of justice, undermining the rule of law. Moreover, the development of the law through the settlement of actual disputes would stop moving forward, leading to a failure to properly resolve human rights issues or to update legal approaches to handling such issues. In the international community, if the standards applied by a nation in the resolution of human rights-related legal disputes remain unchanged and fall short of global standards, the protection of human rights for that nation's citizens will be weaker than is assured in other nations. For these reasons, CLE has increasingly been enhanced and made mandatory in many nations around the world.

Necessity of continuing education

Continuing education to enable attorneys to provide their clients with highest quality legal services is a professional ethical responsibility. At the same time, it is necessary for their business because customers have their choice of legal advisors. Continuing education is also imperative to enable attorneys to increase their international competitiveness in today's globalized world. Training focused on gender issues is an essential component of continuing education to ensure fairness among legal professionals. Currently in Japan, judges, among others, rarely have the opportunity to learn about gender through training programs at the Institute or consultative meetings organized by the Supreme Court Secretariat. For the moment, the more promising 'gender training courses' are arguments, evidence and expert opinions they are exposed to while actually handling cases, namely the on-the-job training by the gender sensitive attorneys.[3] The primary duty of judges is to make final decisions on legal issues. The existence of significant disparities between judges in terms of their overall ability to handle judicial processes, including case management, would adversely affect individuals' human rights and would also undermine public confidence in the judiciary and the legal system, ultimately impeding the development of the law. While litigants assume some responsibility for choosing their attorneys, they cannot choose the judges who will hear their cases. Since the judiciary is funded by taxpayers and judges exercise their authority under a public mandate, a decline in public confidence in judges could undermine public confidence in the judiciary as a whole. In this sense, a higher level of quality assurance is necessary for judges as compared to attorneys, who also provide legal services. Nevertheless, it goes without saying that such quality assurance must not be achieved by exercising direct control over judicial decisions and the decision-making process.

Desirable types of gender training for judges

Judicial independence and public confidence

Judicial independence means the ability of the judiciary to fulfill its function of administering justice, without improper interference or influence from other branches of government. Laws may be products of the political process, but the values embodied by laws – human rights that citizens have attained and the primacy of their universality – must not be influenced by the prevailing political climate. In the modern age, establishing the rule of law and eliminating arbitrary control by politically dominant groups are values that people around the world must pursue. It is the mission of the judiciary to ensure the autonomy of the law and thereby protect human rights. In order to carry out this mission, the judiciary should resist political intervention even when it is claimed to be based on public opinion. This struggle by the judiciary will contribute to strengthening the autonomy of and confidence in the law and ensure tranquility in public life. This should be the foundation of public confidence in the judiciary. To achieve this through the struggle against gender discrimination, gender bias and discriminatory treatment on the basis of gender must be regarded as contrary to the values of the law and dealt with strictly.

How can confidence in the judiciary be secured? In addition to the performance of duties by individual judges – that is, the decisions they hand down in actual cases – their interactions with citizens during the decision-making process are important (Gleeson, 2007). Discrimination in courts on the basis of gender surfaces when citizens detect judges' gender biases and feel that they are being treated unfairly because of gender. Perceptions of gender bias that arise in this manner will shape public opinion regarding judges in general as well as the public's image of the judiciary (Gleeson, 2007). Hence, judicial education ought to include training in the handling of gender issues. In Japan, where the judiciary is characterized by a certain deference to the other branches of government, this is of particular importance in order to demonstrate the professional independence and autonomy of the judiciary as well as of its individual members.

Judicial independence and judicial education

For individual judges, does training constitute interference with their independence or coercion? If training goes so far as to instruct judges how individual cases should be decided, it could not avoid criticism as improper control over judges. The independence of judges and training with regard to their decision-making processes seem to involve a conflict that is extremely difficult to overcome. However, it is also obvious that educational training provided to achieve social justice – a goal to which the entire judiciary should be committed – has value that judges should pursue with sincerity while performing their duties (Wikler, 1989). In common-law countries, training methods have been established based on the assumption that judicial independence and judicial training are compatible. In these countries, judicial training does not give judges suggestions regarding specific cases; rather, it provides judges with references and information that they should take into consideration when trying cases, together with some scientific viewpoints helpful in assessing these materials (Smith, 2005). This approach is intended to support both judges and the judiciary by providing judges with the necessary information and opportunities to improve their capabilities so that they can fulfill their duties more appropriately in accordance with the rule of law and the needs of justice. Provision of knowledge in this manner is thought to be equivalent to the provision of case law information. Therefore, judges are not subject to influence or control in their decision-making processes. How to apply the knowledge they acquire through training is left to their discretion.

Gender training: viewing assumptions skeptically

Gender as a social norm

Gender training must be included in CLE, including judicial education, for the following reasons. Gender is a normative system which affects the everyday actions we take and judgments we make via role expectation, distribution of values and resources, assignment of powers, and imposition of disadvantages. However, since gender is pervasive in our society and considered a given, it can be difficult to see the injustices it causes. Furthermore, the hierarchy or structure of discrimination on the basis of gender can take different forms at different times and places. Therefore, a certain amount of training is necessary in order to enable a person to recognize how casually gender-based discrimination is treated, and to reflect on his/her behavior and modes of thought. This is of course true for judges as well. Judges have superior competence in legal thinking and gain experience through their day-to-day work. Most are extremely earnest and diligent and are eager to perform their duties faithfully. However, although judges are the most professional of the legal professionals in terms of knowledge and legal skill, they cannot learn the above mentioned views on gender or ability to find gender discrimination however closely they look at the law. We all live in society, in accordance with complicated social norms. Judges are no exception. They are also susceptible to ever-present gender bias. To this extent, gender lies at the center of achieving justice.

Necessity of gender training

Unless judicial decisions are based on findings of fact informed by a correct understanding of the social realities, such decisions would tend to go against the weak and worsen their predicaments. Is this compatible with the legal values the judiciary should pursue or the role it should play? Gender norms are so familiar that they often escape notice. If judges could acquire the ability to analyze how they themselves respond to gender norms, they would become capable of identifying society's other opaque control structures which oppress the weak. Reforming these normative systems is indispensable to achieving justice, and if the judiciary, which has been assigned the authority to accomplish this goal, chooses not to take part in reform efforts, it is equivalent to perpetuating society's current power relationships. In addition, the ability to take a skeptical view of the rightness of the existing order leads to the ability to interpret and apply law creatively. Legal professionals who can exercise this ability will be a driving force in the development of the law.

Historically, judicial training on gender began with the women's human rights movements, which made discrimination against women in the law, in courts or among legal professionals a human rights issue. These movements advocated that anti-discrimination measures including legislation would be ineffective without gender awareness of the lawyers, and that it would also be vital for those responsible for enforcement to understand the principles of prohibiting discrimination and that the performance of their duties reflect this understanding (Mahoney, 1996; Minamino, 2012a; Tejima, 2012). For example, if a female attorney is treated with less respect than her male opponent in court, the rights of the citizen who retained her would be ignored, and if a female witness's statement is not given the same level of importance and credibility as that of a male witness, findings of fact would be distorted. A female plaintiff will never be able to vindicate her rights unless she is given the same level of respect in court or by legal professionals as a male defendant. If these instances of discrimination take place repeatedly, discrimination will never be eliminated despite being legally prohibited.

Under the circumstances, even where an anti-discrimination law exists, the values it represents and its legislative objectives will never be achieved, and its effectiveness will never be secured. Women suffer direct disadvantages from ongoing gender discrimination, but this is not the only problem. If the concept of the value of human rights lacks substance, it could disadvantage all people. In addition, negative experiences with the legal process as well as the perception that legislation has failed to effect change could erode public confidence in the law, threatening the rule of law itself.

Activists identified these points and demanded improvements. Their pressure, combined with the judiciary's response, developed into the gender training programs for judges. In the development and introduction of such programs, a private US-based organization created a pioneering program – the National Judicial Education Program (NJEP) (Tejima, 2012), now Legal Momentum (2014). This program was the forerunner of programs later introduced in Canada and Australia (Minamino, 2012c; Takai, 2012). These educational programs consider training to be support for judges and develop curricula which provide judges with a diverse array of information, knowledge and scientific viewpoints that will help them make independent decisions. They also provide judges with the opportunity for self-analysis so that they maintain the appearance of fairness (fairness perceived from a judge's deportment in court). On the other hand, in Germany, a civil-law country, gender training programs have been implemented for judges at both the federal and state levels, with the aim of achieving the same effect.[4] The ideal these training programs seek to foster is a faithful jurist who is willing to learn and self-analyze in an effort to administer justice fairly. Support-based training is possible if this type of judicial autonomy can be relied upon. Here, we can see that if judges cultivate their legal expertise and employ it in achieving justice, people will place confidence in the fairness of the judicial process (Minamino, 2012b).

Problems found with the Japanese judiciary

The committees and councils established as monitoring bodies under international human rights treaties demand that state parties implement training for judges and other legal professionals to ensure that they understand the respective human rights treaties and are able to facilitate fulfillment of the obligations thereunder. Japan, as a state party, is also subject to such demands. For instance, the UN Committee on the Elimination of Discrimination against Women has repeatedly – in fact in every review of reports submitted by the Government of Japan – pointed out in their concluding observations the necessity of implementing training for legal professionals, particularly judges, to ensure their understanding of the CEDAW Convention.[5]

It must be said that Japan's sincerity in fulfilling its obligations in this respect is questionable. The Japanese judiciary has been accused of passivity in applying international human rights law. Even in actions based on international human rights treaties, courts rarely base their decisions on the relevant treaties.[6] According to Yoko Hayashi, a member of the Committee on the Elimination of Discrimination against Women, Japanese judges are unwilling to rely on international human rights law not only because they lack adequate knowledge of it,[7] but also because they receive insufficient training on it. She also stated that due to this attitude on the part of judges, Japanese citizens enjoy a lower level of human rights protection than the global standard and further, that Japan has been unable to participate in the development of human rights law taking place among countries which emphasize human rights (Hayashi, 2013). Thus, Japanese citizens are at an extremely serious double disadvantage. The current situation in which the protection of human rights for Japanese women falls behind the global standard must be rectified.

The judiciary could secure its independence by making decisions based on international human rights standards. Doing so would insulate them from pressure by other government branches on the basis of universal values of the law. This is also vital if Japan is to fulfill its ethical responsibilities as a developed country.

While Japanese courts emphasize judicial independence, they have not sought to ground independence in the attention paid to or support for it provided for citizens.[8] The Japanese judiciary has not ensured judges' independence by providing them with support-based training. To put it another way, it has not respected judges' autonomous decisions or provided them with the materials and viewpoints necessary to make such decisions. Rather, as mentioned earlier, the Supreme Court Secretariat has suggested specific conclusions and has thus exercised control over the outcome of litigation. This is a problem with the judicial bureaucracy and it too must be rectified.

In contrast, German judges, who operate under a career system similar to that of Japanese judges, are not considered to be subject to such control. This is a problem specific to the Japanese judiciary and not to the career system. The gender training implemented in Germany – although not a comprehensive program – is purported to have the same goal as the gender training programs of Canada and Australia. This demonstrates that support-based training for professionals is not incompatible with the career system. It is possible to introduce support-based training to the Japanese judiciary, and this attempt has the potential to build new relationships between the judiciary and individual judges, and between the judiciary and the public.

The difference between the Japanese judiciary and the judiciaries of other developed countries requiring the most attention is the relative homogeneity of the Japanese bench. This is due to Japan's relative lack of diversity in terms of ethnicity and language and the fact that students who choose to be judges are concentrated in certain social classes. In this respect, the biases of the majority are liable to be more widespread, reducing the opportunity for individual judges to recognize their own biases. Judges, like all people, have various biases, and with this in mind, judicial education should be carried out according to the basic belief that judges can try to eliminate their biases through their own efforts. Judges must admit and examine their own biases as part of the process of interpreting the law. This attitude will define the extent to which judges are legally allowed to assert their individuality. As a first step, it is necessary to introduce gender issues in judicial education in Japan. Doing so could be expected to have a significant effect in every respect.

If the judiciary wishes to emphasize the independence of individual judges and support the independence of the judiciary as a whole, it should adopt a training method that respects the autonomy of judges. The public believes that judges have or pursue the potential for circumspection and can improve their attitudes and behaviors to be more fair and appropriate to achieving justice. The public's attention to and criticism of judicial decisions can be seen as a sign of its expectations for and confidence in the courts. We can support and cooperate with the courts when they take required actions. When we are convinced that courts have met our expectations and responded to our concerns, we will have deeper confidence in courts, further strengthening the foundations of judicial independence. The Japanese judiciary should have the courage to place its trust in the people.

Disclosure statement

No potential conflict of interest was reported by the author.

Funding

This work was supported by JSPS Grants-in-Aid for Scientific Research [grant number 20330033].

Notes

[1] Of Japan's 72 law schools, 32 responded to the survey on gender law and gender education conducted at the end of 2012 by the Gender Law Committee of the Science Council of Japan. A gender-related subject was included in the curricula of 13 respondent law schools, two of which set it as a mandatory two-credit subject.

[2] *Shirafuji et al.* v. *Sumitomo Denki Kyogyo Co.*, Osaka District Court 31 July 2000, case no. Heisei(wa) 8009.

[3] On 14 June 2014, the Committee on Equality of Men and Women of the Japan Federation of Bar Associations held a symposium to advocate the necessity of systematic and uniform implementation of gender training, and prepared a textbook for such training.

[4] On 13 April 2014, the International Workshop for Gender-Fair Judiciary was held as an event funded by Grants-in-Aid for Scientific Research. Instructors were invited from a common-law countries and a civil-law country to give trial lessons to Japanese practitioners and researchers. The workshops given by the gender training instructor in judicial education from the civil-law country (Germany) differed from that given by the judicial education instructor specialized in the subject of gender from the common-law country in terms of the theoretical basis of the training programs, but they were basically the same in substance. Both workshops were helpful to participants in identifying and recognizing the gender norms and biases in everyday life.

[5] In particular, in its review of the 2001 report, when the aforementioned *Sumitomo Denki Kyogyo* case was pending before the Osaka High Court, the Committee on the Elimination of Discrimination against Women demanded implementation of training for legal professionals, while specifically explaining to the Government of Japan the understanding of the doctrine of indirect discrimination. In addition, Japan has also been urged by the United Nations Commission on Human Rights, upon review of every report submitted by the Government of Japan, to ensure a thorough understanding of international human rights covenants among legal professionals by providing training.

[6] Recently the Kyoto District Court (decision on 8 November 2013) and the Osaka High Court (decision on 8 July 2014) found that the obstreperous campaign recently carried out by a citizens group against a Korean school and its students constituted hate speech prohibited under the International Convention on the Elimination of All Forms of Racial Discrimination. The court relied on this convention because there is no legislation in Japan that directly addresses hate speech.

[7] This lack of knowledge has been attributed to the fact that students pay little attention to international law because it is not a major subject of the bar examination and does not need to be studied to pass the examination. Another reason may be that legal practitioners have paid little attention to international human rights because courts rarely make mention of it.

[8] The Supreme Court defines the characteristics or virtues of the Japanese judiciary to be a unified system and to offer homogenous judicial services – in other words, unity in the conclusions of the judicial system in the twenty-first century: See Judicial Reform Council (2001) and also Minamino (2013, p. 547).

References

Gleeson, M. (2007) Public Confidence in the Courts, National Judicial College of Australia. Available at: http://www.hcourt.gov.au/assets/publications/speeches/former-justices/gleesoncj/cj_9feb07.pdf, accessed October 31, 2011.

Hayashi, Y. (2013) Implementation of the Convention on the Elimination of All Forms of Discrimination against Women in Japan, *Journal of East Asia and International*, 2, pp. 341–366.

Judicial Reform Council. (2001) A report to the Judicial Reform Council S.Ct. Available at: www.courts.go.jp/about/kaikaku_sihou-21.html, accessed September 15, 2014.

Legal Momentum: The Women's Legal Defence and Education Fund. (2014) Available at: https://www.legalmomentum.org/, accessed September 15, 2014.

Mahoney, K. (1996) The myth of judicial neutrality: the role of judicial education in the fair administration of justice, Willamette Law Review, 32, pp. 785–820.

Minamino, K. (2012a)* Coping with perceived 'Gender Bias in the Courts' through judicial education, *Sociology of Law*, 77, pp. 107–133.

Minamino, K. (2012b)* Gender fairness and continuing legal education, in: K. Minamino (Ed) *Comparative Research on Continuing Legal Education* (Tokyo, Nihon Kajo Shuppan), pp. 267–277.

Minamino, K. (2012c)* Gender and continuing judicial education in Australia, in: K. Minamino (Ed) *Comparative Research on Continuing Legal Education* (Tokyo, Nihon Kajo Shuppan), pp. 77–97.

Minamino, K. (2013) Gender and judging in Japan, in: U. Schultz & G. Shaw (Eds) *Gender and Judging* (London, Hart Publishing), pp. 543–555.

Miyazawa, S. & Kisa, S. (2009)* Judicial administrative control over judges in Japan, in: S. Kisa, S. Miyazawa, T. Sato, S. Kawashima, N. Mizutani, K. Ageishi (Eds) *Japanese Judicial System*, 5th ed (Tokyo, Nihon Hyouron Sha), pp. 188–212.

Sato, I. (2000*) The consistency and inconsistency (uneinheitlichkeit) of the judiciary, *Sociology of Law*, 53, pp. 146–163.

Science Council of Japan. (2014)* Report on Gender Law Courses in Legal Education, paper presented at *Science Council of Japan Symposium on Law and Gender: Can We Change the Legislature and the Judiciary?* Waseda University, 28 June.

Smith, L. (2005) Judicial Education on Context, *University of British Columbia Law Review*, 38(2), pp. 569–582.

Takai, H. (2012)* Gender and continuing legal education in Canada, in: K. Minamino (Ed) *Comparative Research on Continuing Legal Education* (Tokyo, Nihon Kajo Shuppan), pp. 61–75.

Tejima, A. (2012)* Gender and continuing legal education in U.S., in: K. Minamino (Ed) *Comparative Research on Continuing Legal* Education (Tokyo, Nihon Kajo Shuppan), pp. 35–60.

Watanabe, C. (2015) Japanese judicial education: working toward gender equality in the judiciary, *International Journal of Legal Profession*, doi:10.1080/09695958.2015.1029486.

Wikler, N. (1989) Water on stone: a perspective on the movement to eliminate gender bias in the courts, *Court Review*, Fall, pp. 9–26.

*Originally Japanese title translated into English for this publication only.

Japanese judicial education: working toward gender equality in the judiciary

CHIHARA WATANABE
Faculty of Law, Ritsumeikan University, Kyoto, Japan

ABSTRACT *The Japanese judiciary on the whole has been passive and conservative, with a tendency to make uniform decisions. It has also long been criticized for its gender bias. While isolation from the general public enables Japanese judges to maintain their impartiality, it has also made their decisions more susceptible to being influenced by their personal values and biases. The process of bringing about order between private persons sometimes requires an aggressive attempt to develop legal doctrines, and in this respect, there may be room for a judiciary that is responsive to gender issues.*

The Japanese judiciary has never made a systematic effort to address gender issues. Within the framework of judicial education, gender issues are addressed only as the topic of a lecture delivered by an outside instructor in a class on general or international human rights. In light of this current situation, as well as signs of a slightly active movement in the Japanese judiciary following the ongoing justice system reforms initiated in 2000, I explore a possible approach to making the Japanese judiciary more responsive to gender issues.

The Japanese judiciary and gender issues

The Japanese judiciary has never given primary importance to gender-related issues or tried to tackle them systematically. In some actual cases, the courts have taken the lead in developing legal doctrines conducive to gender equality. However, due to the judiciary's conservative nature and a lack of understanding of judges, court decisions often accept societal gender bias as a given or overlook serious gender discrimination, perpetuating or worsening the problem.

To consider the judiciary's efforts to cope with gender issues, it is first necessary to pay attention to the characteristics of the Japanese justice system and Japanese judicial culture.

The Japanese justice system and judicial culture

The Japanese judiciary has not been subject to any significant political influence and has long been criticized as passive and conservative. The liberal post-war atmosphere that prevailed following the introduction of the judicial review system derived from the United States of America saw a few cases in which district courts ruled the Self-Defense Forces to be unconstitutional. However, under pressure from the government of that time, Japanese courts began to avoid making independent decisions in highly political cases.[1] The Supreme Court of Japan has ruled laws and regulations to be unconstitutional in only nine cases since the end of the war 70 years ago.

In its recruitment of judges, the Japanese judiciary has adopted the career system imported from continental law countries; that is, an apprenticeship system in which assistant judges are appointed from among young apprentices who have passed the national bar examination. Because the court system is a centralized, bureaucratic organization with the Supreme Court at the top, the Secretariat of the Supreme Court has in effect exercised control over personnel affairs and thereby achieved a judiciary so homogenous that the same decision can be expected by any court in Japan.[2] Courts are unwilling to disclose information on their internal workings, likely due to a desire to maintain this system. Secrecy is another characteristic of the Japanese judiciary.

Japanese courts have demonstrated their political neutrality by standing apart from society and refraining from taking part in any political activities. In 1970, the Supreme Court refused to re-appoint an assistant judge who belonged to the Japan Young Lawyers Association.[3] Then Chief Justice of the Supreme Court Kazuto Ishida, in his address at the new year's meeting, stated, "The 'fairness' of judges does not only require that their decisions be fair; it also requires that the public believe with confidence that judges are fair" (Ishida, 1970) and "judges must be careful about every action they take in every sphere of their private lives and must try to avoid being viewed with suspicion by the public in any respect" (Ishida, 1970).

At the same time, Japanese judges have traditionally been expected to resolve disputes with great sagacity, not only by finding formally appropriate legal solutions but also by paying attention to the social context and background of each case. This idealized conception of judges may be reflected in the statue of Themis at the entrance of the Supreme Court of Japan. While other statues of Themis often show her blindfolded, symbolizing the need to avoid bias, this statue depicts Themis with her eyes open, so that she can see everything.

Thus, Japanese judges are required to maintain strict political neutrality, refrain from contact with society, try cases with keen insight, and make decisions based on common sense. Taken as a whole, these requirements are basically designed to maintain a stable and uniform legal order. This judicial culture is said to be rooted in the relatively homogenous Japanese society and culture and is attributed to the fact that judges share communitarian and consensus-oriented social values (Halay, 2011).

However, the Japanese courts cannot be accused of remaining conservative or passive in all categories of cases. They have, in fact, played an active role in developing new legal doctrines with the support of social consensus in civil disputes – e.g. by awarding relief to victims of pollution – thereby taking the lead in Japanese society

(Foote, 2006). They have even been said to "play an activist role" when compared to courts in the US (Upham, 2011). The common practice adopted by the Japanese judiciary is to formulate legal norms using flexible interpretations of general clauses in the Civil Code – namely, the public order clause – and by relying on general social acceptability.

The Japanese judiciary's responses to gender issues

The Constitution of Japan goes beyond the international average in its response to gender issues, advocating substantial gender equality and expressly prohibiting gender-based discrimination, although only within the context of family relationships. It is true that positive law, such as the Civil Code, does not adequately achieve gender equality, but efforts have been made to catch up with international norms with respect to positive law as well. In 1985, the *Act on Securing, Etc. of Equal Opportunity and Treatment between Men and Women in Employment* (Equal Employment Opportunity Act) was enacted, upon which Japan ratified the Convention on the Elimination of All Forms of Discrimination against Women. The *Basic Act for Gender Equal Society and the Act on the Prevention of Spousal Violence* and the *Protection of Victims* (Domestic Violence Prevention Act) were then enacted in 1999 and 2001, respectively.

Where the positive law system was incomplete, the Japanese judiciary in some cases aggressively attempted to develop legal doctrines to fill the gaps. This was probably because gender issues were perceived to be less political and thus suitable for judicial law making. For example, in 1966, the Tokyo District Court found that a provision in an employment contract that forced women to leave employment upon marriage or reaching the age of 35 constituted unreasonable and discriminatory treatment on the basis of gender, and ruled this provision to be contrary to public order and therefore void under Article 90 of the Civil Code.[4]

In response to this and other disputes arising from gender discrimination in employment, courts to a certain extent found appropriate solutions by developing their own legal doctrines. The Equal Employment Opportunity Act enacted in 1985 can be said to incorporate these legal doctrines.

However, the development of legal doctrines through the interpretation of general clauses in this manner largely depends on the discretion of individual judges. And due to the conservative nature of the Japanese judiciary as a whole, judges are liable to affirm the status quo of gender inequality in society. In the field of labor law, discrimination against women in promotions was found not to be against public order on the basis of the circumstances of the time, such as prevailing social attitudes and the average length of service by female employees, thus justifying the discriminatory practice.[5]

This gender bias causes problems across all fields of law, and is particularly likely to result in serious problems when associated with violence against women. In the early 1990s, the courts found sexual harassment to be a tort and upheld victims' claims for damages against their harassers. This was recognized to be the development of a new legal doctrine by the judiciary. Subsequently, however, the existence of sexual harassment was denied in a series of court decisions under the logic that can only be described as a rapist's myth: that it is unnatural for women "to have neither run away, nor complained immediately", after their bosses' sexual assaults, which were in many cases nearly equivalent to rape. Furthermore, in divorce cases involving domestic violence, women are often told by judges or counselors that it is their fault that they were beaten by their husbands. Even after the Domestic Violence Prevention Act entered into force, the courts have been repeatedly criticized for not issuing protection orders swiftly in serious cases.

Japan has been attacked for this by the international community. Although Japan has ratified the Convention on the Elimination of All Forms of Discrimination against Women, it has yet to domestically implement the Convention to the fullest extent. The legislative branch has been slow in responding to repeated requests to take corrective measures, such as amending discriminatory provisions that remain in the Civil Code. There has also been a call for the Japanese judiciary to enhance judicial implementation of the Convention and become more aware of this issue. However, Japanese courts have not, to date, been active in the domestic implementation of international conventions.

Has justice system reform changed Japanese judicial culture?

The passivity of the Japanese judiciary began to come under fire in the 1990s not only from the bar, but also from the business community and citizens' groups. "Preposterous decisions made by judges who know nothing about the world outside the court" were targeted for criticism. Bar associations and societies of law argued forcefully that the root of the problem was the judiciary's excessive bureaucratization. In order to break this down, these groups advocated reforms to the justice system such as abolishing the existing career system and introducing a unified legal profession system from common-law countries and also a jury or lay assessor system along the lines of the German *Schoeffengericht*. The Justice System Reform Council, established by the Cabinet in 1999, discussed a wide range of issues, leading to the most radical justice system reforms of the post-war period.

Based on the recommendations submitted by the Council to the Cabinet in 2001, law schools were established in 2004 to substantially increase the number of legal professionals. In 2009, the lay judge system was introduced to enable the "sound social common sense of the people" to be reflected in the adjudication of serious criminal cases. Under this system, lay judges (called *saiban-in*) elected from among the general public are assigned, in collaboration with professional judges, to make findings of fact and determine sentences in serious criminal cases. In addition to these drastic changes, a system of enlisting the cooperation of experts was established to help judges handle lawsuits in specialized fields, such as medical malpractice cases, which were increasing at the time. Taken as a whole, the reforms were intended to increase judicial capacity and bring the judiciary closer to the people, while responding to the criticism of "preposterous" court decisions by introducing ideas that have achieved general social acceptability as well as the specialized knowledge of experts into the judicial decision-making process.

However, only limited reforms were made to the judicial profession. The career system was maintained, and the development of a system enabling assistant judges to experience other jobs was the only response taken to the criticism that judges "know nothing about the world outside the court". Gender issues were not addressed[6] and no special reforms were made in this regard. Thus, even after the justice system reforms are completed, there is little hope that the judicial circumstances will change dramatically in terms of gender issues.

Nevertheless, we have seen signs of change in the Japanese judiciary since the justice system reforms began. For example, four out of the nine post-war court rulings finding legislation unconstitutional have been made since 2000. Decisions were rendered holding as unconstitutional the *Nationality Act* of 2008,[7] and the inheritance law in the Civil Code that discriminated against children born out of wedlock in terms of their statutory shares in inheritance (2013). They were declared to constitute breaches of the principle of equality under Article 14 of the Constitution. Legislative action to revise the relevant provisions was taken soon after these decisions were issued.

Worth noting in these rulings is that the court took into account the change in the legislative fact that the distinction by law between children born in and out of wedlock was no longer reasonable due to changes in the general social acceptability of various types of families and parent–child relationships as well as changes in other social circumstances. The court also made reference to legislative trends in other countries and international treaties ratified by Japan.

More specifically, in its 2013 Grand Bench decision, the Supreme Court ruled that the provision in the Civil Code setting the statutory inheritance share of a child born out of wedlock as one half that of a child born in wedlock breached the principle of equality, holding as follows:

> Giving comprehensive consideration to circumstances such as the trends in society seen from the time of the 1947 Civil Code revision up until now, the diversification of the forms of family in Japan and the changes in people's perceptions resulting therefrom, the legislative trends in other countries as well as the content of the treaties ratified by Japan and the criticism given by the committees set up under these treaties, the changes in the legal system, etc. relating to the distinction between children born in wedlock and children born out of wedlock, and the problems, etc. repeatedly pointed out in the rulings handed down by this court thus far, it can be said to be an evident fact that respect for individuals in a family, which is a collective unit, has been recognized more clearly.[8]

The "legislative fact" discussed here was not examined in detail based on evidence of social facts as it should have been according to the legislative fact theory, and the international treaties ratified by Japan were treated only as one matter to be taken into account when assessing the legislative fact. In this respect, the theoretical process employed by the Supreme Court was a more conventional approach, relying on general social acceptability. Still, the fact that the Supreme Court touched on the legislative fact theory and the relevance of international treaties in its rulings finding legislation unconstitutional – which could have a great impact – can be understood as a sign that the judiciary is becoming more responsive to gender issues.

The ongoing justice system reforms do not directly address gender issues and we cannot expect them to bring about fundamental solutions to these issues. Nevertheless, enhanced involvement of ordinary people and experts in the judicial process could remind a homogenous group of judges of their own gender biases, making it possible that the increasingly active judiciary could become more responsive to gender issues.

Before discussing this in detail, I will review the judicial training and research programs provided for judges at the Legal Training and Research Institute and the treatment of gender issues in these programs.

Gender issues in judicial training

The judicial training system

While judges basically learn judicial practices through on-the-job training in what are in essence apprenticeships, they also receive formal training at the Legal Training and Research Institute (the LTRI; hereinafter the 'Institute'). The Institute, which is an organization affiliated with the Supreme Court, is responsible for training candidates for the legal profession and provides training and research programs for judges. It is also said to play a role in maintaining the uniformity of the Japanese judiciary.

Training and research programs for judges have the official objective of providing judges with the opportunity to receive organized training programs in order to, "gain diverse and abundant knowledge and experience".[9] Specifically, the following types of programs are provided: (1) introductory training courses upon appointment as judges or assumption of new duties or posts, by having all eligible trainees gather at the Institute; (2) field-specific workshops for each area of jurisprudence to enable judges to study topics in their chosen fields; (3) comprehensive workshops for research on various issues faced by courts; and (4) dispatch-style training courses.

Introductory training courses are mandatory for all judges, and are divided into the following: (1) training courses for newly appointed assistant judges; (2) basic training courses for assistant judges; (3) workshops for newly appointed judges; (4) workshops for chiefs of branch offices and for the presiding judges of divisions; and (5) practical workshops for attorneys appointed as judges. Each course or workshop lasts for three–four days, during which trainees mainly seek to acquire knowledge and skills in relation to practical techniques and laws necessary to perform their newly assigned duties. Newly appointed judges also study judicial administration and trial management. These training programs place greater emphasis on the practical objective of enabling judges to acquire knowledge and skills necessary for performing their duties than they do on achieving the officially stated purpose of enabling judges to acquire, "diverse and abundant knowledge and experience". These programs mostly consist of lectures by internal instructors, such as staff from the Supreme Court Secretariat's Personnel Affairs and General Affairs Bureaus.

Two types of field-specific workshops are provided: (1) basic field workshops which address the basic areas of law, such as civil, criminal, domestic relations and juvenile law; and (2) specialized field workshops designed to provide knowledge in specialized fields, including administrative, labor, intellectual property, medical and tax law. Each workshop lasts for about three days for judges assigned to handle cases in the respective fields.

Judges also engage in research[10] on important issues in judicial practice. Recent research topics have included the operation of the lay judge system, the use of scientific evidence in trials, and findings of fact on contractual matters in civil cases. Gender issues, which extend across a wide range of legal fields, have not been chosen as a research topic.

In addition, the Institute also organizes multidisciplinary training programs in fields not directly related to legal practice to enable judges to acquire broader views and deeper insight. These programs address various issues, including environmental problems, regenerative medicine and health issues. They take a variety of forms, such as lectures, panel discussions and round-table meetings. However, gender issues have not been chosen in these programs either.

While the official objective of these group training programs at the Institute is to enable judges to acquire, "diverse and abundant knowledge and experience", they are actually centered on enabling judges to acquire knowledge and skills necessary for judicial practice. Introductory training courses, which are mandatory for all judges are considered particularly important contributors to the integrity and homogeneity of the judiciary. Furthermore, as the period for group training at the Institute has been shortened,[11] fewer opportunities are likely to exist for introducing more programs providing a greater variety of knowledge and experience.

Meanwhile, dispatch-style training programs have been enhanced. This type of training was advocated by former Chief Justice Koichi Yaguchi in the late 1980s, as evidenced by his statement that, "Before being jurists, judges must be good members of society who have sound common sense" (Yaguchi, 1993). During these programs, judges attend training at private corporations, media organizations and the Bank of Japan. Judges and assistant judges specialized in handling cases relating to intellectual property rights are assigned to receive special training in this field. Short-term training programs last from two to three weeks and long-term programs from two to three months.

The overseas study program has also been enhanced. When first introduced in 1972, only a few judges were given the chance to study abroad. Today, as a result of the justice system reforms, about 35 judges are sent to Europe, the United States and Australia every year to study for one or two years. Since the introduction of the system enabling assistant judges to experience other jobs in 2005, assistant judges have also been given the opportunity to experience work outside court and to study overseas.

Gender issues in judicial training

An outline of the judicial training programs is provided on the Supreme Court's website, but detailed information on these programs – specifically, their treatment of gender issues – has not been available and has remained unknown. I therefore investigated the treatment of gender issues by analyzing information obtained from questionnaires I sent to the Institute in 2009 and 2014 and from telephone interviews.[12]

I learned that a 90–150 minute lecture on human rights in general or international human rights is offered as part of the introductory training course curriculum for judges, and that gender issues are addressed during this lecture.

Gender issues covered in these lectures "to increase judges' awareness of human rights" include domestic violence, sexual harassment, the Convention on the Elimination of All Forms of Discrimination Against Women, reproductive health, etc. Thus, gender issues are discussed as one human rights issue among many. While group training at the Institute is basically conducted by internal instructors, human rights training is mainly conducted by invited, outside instructors, who also determine the specifics of the training.

There has been criticism that the manner in which judges handle cases involving domestic violence, among other gender issues, shows the judiciary's gender bias. However, domestic violence cases have not been chosen as an independent subject for group training because it is not considered to be a human rights issue.

The main goal of the mandatory introductory training courses is to enable judges to acquire the minimum level of practical knowledge and skills required, and there is little hope that gender issues will be addressed via these training courses. Conversely, gender issues are unlikely to be covered in field-specific workshops because the workshops emphasize highly practical and specialized topics. Gender issues have also never been addressed in general education training. Thus, the judiciary does not have the mindset to include gender issues within the scope of the topics that judges must learn in order to acquire "diverse and abundant knowledge and experience".

In my view, gender education for judges is insufficient. But there might be hope for improvement. When I asked why the Institute chooses to offer at least one class on human rights every year as part of the curriculum, the interviewee answered, "Human rights is an important issue, and if a class on human rights is not included in the curriculum every year, some judges might miss the chance to hear a lecture on this topic". This answer demonstrates how group training both reflects and contributes to the uniformity of the Japanese judiciary. The fact that human rights issues are addressed in training programs that judges should attend periodically according to their length of service – even as the topic of only one lecture class – is significant at least in that it represents the Supreme Court's belief that human rights is an essential topic which it affords all judges the opportunity to learn.

At present, 'human rights' is the point of connection through which gender issues might be able to find a place in judicial training. Accordingly, it may be necessary to seek their inclusion based on jurisprudence: i.e. by researching gender issues in society and recasting them as human rights issues.[13]

Possible approaches to making the judiciary more responsive to gender issues

In light of the current situation, I will provide some ideas regarding possible approaches to encourage judges to create law in response to gender issues and for the direction that judicial education should take to implement these approaches.

Social consensus approach

Justifying attempts by judges to create law by social consensus – the basis of Japanese judicial culture – is still the most popular approach. Throughout the history of the Japanese courts, judges have been authorized to create law by interpreting the general clauses of the Civil Code or incorporating ideas that achieved general social acceptability in order to resolve disputes between private persons. In the future, they are likely to continue to rely on concepts such as 'public order' and 'general social acceptability' as formal grounds for justifying the legal doctrines they develop.

'General social acceptability' is considered to be a type of norm that cannot be reduced to mere social facts. When judges rely on general social acceptability, they try to extrapolate a social consensus from the facts in accordance with their own consciences and render judgment from a normative perspective. This is the most prospective approach to the creation of law, and is also likely to be affected by the personal views (e.g. gender biases) of individual judges. The risk of a bias held by elite adult men working in a conservative and insular environment cannot be ruled out.

In order to maintain judges' impartiality, the Japanese judiciary has adopted a bureaucratic structure to achieve uniformity and has sought to reduce the amount of direct contact judges have with ordinary society to prevent them from being unduly influenced by lay people. Judicial training programs in Canada and Australia have not directly asserted that judges have gender biases. Rather they have been designed to enable judges to gain, "diverse and abundant knowledge and experience", and not to correct or eliminate bias (Smith, 2005). Even so, this approach involves transformation of the judicial culture – a difficult challenge that even the justice system reforms have not overcome. As judicial omnipotence is nothing more than a myth, the judicial authorities should sincerely admit that judges are susceptible to biases that can be moderated by wider understandings introduced through systematic training programs. For example, judicial educational schemes implemented in Australia and Canada should be introduced in Japan.

Because such an approach may be indirect, I propose two alternative approaches that may yield more immediate results. The first is premised on courts taking into account legislative facts when finding legislation unconstitutional in recent cases. The second approach would treat gender issues as a subset of international human rights and thus appropriately considered in depth as part of education in that area.

Legislative fact approach

A legislative fact is a general social, economic, cultural or scientific fact that provides a basis for the enactment of a law and that makes the law reasonable. While legislative facts are usually examined during judicial review, courts may also use these facts as a basis for developing new legal doctrines through litigation in order to clarify underlying social facts (Hara, 2000). In the United States, evidence on matters of social science is often used to craft epochal rulings. In Japan, courts have traditionally allowed the legislative branch broad discretion, but in recent constitutionality cases, the reasonableness of a law has been denied on the grounds of a change in the legislative facts. This is a new approach to the creation of law.

The legislative fact approach controls the process of creating law through litigation and leads it in an appropriate direction based on the facts. In this respect, it is superior to the social consensus approach that relies on the personal recognition of individual judges. It also has the potential to enable feminist arguments and a wide range of other social science topics to be incorporated into the reasoning for the creation of law. This approach aligns with the trend of respecting expertise exemplified by the justice system reforms. In particular, it may be an effective means of introducing expertise on issues not amenable to the application of conventional wisdom, such as domestic violence and sexual crime.

However, this approach also involves a risk of overreliance on statistical data of dubious significance or of accepting the status quo on the basis of social facts that only reflect society's inherent gender inequality, such as statistical data indicating that only a small number of women hold managerial posts. To avoid these risks, in addition to promoting the legislative fact approach, it is necessary for gender studies scholars to actively present research results that would be useful in this approach.

International human rights approach

Academically, the international treaties Japan has ratified and promulgated under Article 98 of the Constitution are effective domestically and have precedence over national law. But Japanese courts have not been active in interpreting human rights treaties to which Japan is a contracting party or in applying them in domestic litigation.

In connection with this, it is worth noting that the Supreme Court has mentioned international human rights treaties and recommendations based on them in its recent unconstitutionality rulings. As gender issues permeate all aspects of society, in identifying them as problems to solve we can learn a lot from international perspectives, particularly the Convention on the Elimination of All Forms of Discrimination against Women and the recommendations made by the Committee on the Elimination of Discrimination against Women. Therefore, it is vital to promote the domestic implementation of international human rights treaties.

Training at the Institute, which addresses gender issues only as part of a single lecture on human rights in general or international human rights, is insufficient to achieve recognition of the significance of gender equality. However, this lecture is important in that it provides all judges with an opportunity to learn about international human rights treaties at the Institute, which is affiliated with the Supreme Court, thereby raising awareness of these treaties and the norms that they represent. It must at least be ensured that this lecture class remains part of the training curriculum.

Conclusion

There is a limit to what can be achieved through the training provided to judges. Attitudes and bias are not generated overnight and cannot be corrected in a day. Since the Institute cannot solve the problem alone, education at law schools takes on additional importance. Even so, in view of the monolithic, insular judicial culture of Japan, training for judges may bring about a greater than expected effect. Hence, it is absolutely necessary to improve judicial training programs.

Meanwhile, as a result of the justice system reforms, the size of the Japanese legal profession has increased, and the number of women in the legal profession has also increased.[14] While the group training period at the Institute has been shortened, opportunities for judges to participate in external training or to study overseas have actually increased, albeit only slightly. There has been progress, however halting and inadequate, toward releasing judges from their closed and controlled environment and encouraging them to acquire diverse experience outside courts. It is not yet clear how these trends toward opening up the judiciary will affect its responsiveness to gender issues, but I do hope that they bring change to a judicial culture which is currently closed, conservative and plagued by gender bias.

Disclosure statement

No potential conflict of interest was reported by the author.

Funding

This work is supported by The Grants-in-Aid for Scientific Research [Grant number 25285005].

Notes

[1] Typical examples of highly political cases are those challenging the constitutionality of the Self-Defense Force and the Japan–US Security Treaty. For example, in its judgment in the Sunagawa Case in 1959, the Grand Bench of the Supreme Court reversed a district court ruling that had found the stationing of US troops to be unconstitutional. Under a theory which is close to the theory of *acte de gouvernement*, the top court clearly showed its tendency to refrain from judicial review of the issue in dispute, holding that, "the Security Treaty is ... of highly political nature ... and unless it is found to be obviously unconstitutional and void, it falls outside the scope of matters subject to this court's judicial review authority".

[2] Half a year after the Judicial System Reform Council initiated discussions in 1999, the Supreme Court submitted to it a report arguing against the proposals of the pro-reform group to introduce

a unified legal profession system and jury system. In this report, the Supreme Court expressed the view that the integrity of the justice system and the homogeneity of judicial practice respond to the desires of a very homogenous Japanese society. The Supreme Court also stressed that in order to achieve a uniform, homogenous judiciary, it is necessary to maintain a justice system operated by career judges appointed under the career system.

[3] In the late 1960s, Japan entered a period of judicial crisis, when courts became increasingly conservative and passive under pressure from the government that was opposed to liberal court decisions. In the early 1970s, this emerged in the form of attacks on judges who belonged to the Japan Young Lawyers Association (an autonomous study group of young jurists), such as urging judges to leave the association or refusing to re-appoint an assistant judge who was a member of the association.

[4] *Suzuki* v. *Sumitomo Semento Co., Tokyo District Court,* 20 December 1966.

[5] *Shirafuji et al* v. *Sumitomo Denki Kyogyo Co.,* Osaka District Court, 31 July 2000. This case concluded with a settlement before the High Court, which was basically in favor of the plaintiffs' position. This was largely thanks to an active campaign against the defendant, such as the submission of opinions critical of its position by many scholars.

[6] Despite the request from the Japan Federation of Bar Associations, the recommendations submitted by the Council made no mention of a proposal from the gender perspective.

[7] Judgment ruling the Nationality Act to be unconstitutional, rendered by the Grand Bench of the Supreme Court, on 4 June 2008.

[8] The Grand Bench of the Supreme Court, 4 September 2013, 2012 (Ku) No. 984 and 985, *Minshu* Vol. 67, No. 6.

[9] http://www.courts.go.jp/saikosai/sihokensyujo/saibankankensyu/index.html (last accessed 30 May 2014).

[10] Joint research conducted with the goal of compiling the research results into a report to be completed in the coming year.

[11] For example, in 2005, newly appointed assistant judges underwent eight days of training and assistant judges received five days of training in the second year of their service. This has been reduced to four days and three days, respectively.

[12] In light of the conventional, secretive nature of the courts, it is considered difficult for them to answer these kinds of questions. The fact that I received some replies can be seen as a positive result of the justice system reforms.

[13] The Japan Association of Gender and Law was inaugurated in 2003. However, this was after the commencement of the justice system reforms. The failure to include gender issues in the scope of official issues for reform indicates that we were late to begin the process of achieving gender equality in the judiciary.

[14] The legal profession doubled in size in the past decade and the proportion of female judges surpassed 20 percent.

References

Foote, D.H. (2006) *The Judiciary and Society: Reconsidering the "Myth" about the Judiciary* [Saiban to Shakai: Shiho no "Joshiki" Saiko]. (Tokyo, NTT Shuppan).

Halay, J.O. (2011) Constitutional adjudication in Japan: context, structures, and values, *Washington University Law Review,* 88, pp. 1467–1491.

Hara, T. (2000) *Saiban-niyoru Housouzou to Jijitsushinri* (Tokyo, Kobundo).

Ishida, K. (1970) Shinnen-no Kotoba, Saibansho-jiho, 536, p. 1.

Smith, L. (2005) Judicial Education on context, *University on British Columbia Law Review,* 38, pp. 569–582.

Upham, F.K. (2011) Stealth activism: norm formation by Japanese courts, *Washington University Law Review,* 88, pp. 1493–1505.

Yaguchi, K. (1993) *Saiko-Saibansho to Tomoni* (Tokyo, Yuhikaku).

Gender stereotypes and attitudes within the judiciary of Bosnia and Herzegovina: a case for increased awareness and education

HEATHER HUHTANEN* & MAJDA HALILOVIĆ**

Gender and Security Program, DCAF, Geneva, Switzerland

***Research and Policy, The Atlantic Initiative, Sarajevo, Bosnia and Herzegovina*

ABSTRACT *Judges, prosecutors, attorneys and other court personnel bring their academic training, professional experience, legal diligence and good intentions to their work; they also bring their values, beliefs and opinions. The concept of gender is among those strongly influenced by cultural perspectives and is therefore a potential source of bias, affecting interactions among and between court professionals and court users. This article reflects on the findings of the first research effort aimed at identifying and examining the influence of gender within the judiciary of Bosnia and Herzegovina (BiH). The views and opinions of 161 respondents – judges, prosecutors, attorneys and court associates in BiH – were captured through an anonymous online questionnaire and in-person interviews. Previous scholarship from North America and Europe is used to analyse the findings and to identify gender-related stereotypes and attitudes present within the BiH judiciary. This article concludes by arguing that if the BiH judiciary wishes to deliver fair and impartial justice, judicial reform efforts will need to prioritize gender awareness education and address the issue of gender bias.*

Introduction

Research on how legal practitioners influence the implementation of laws has been undertaken for decades (Falk Moore, 1978; Merry, 1986; Shehada, 2005; Rosen, 2008). For example, Sally Falk Moore, a legal anthropologist who has published extensively on cross-cultural, comparative legal theory found that regardless of the legal system, context or the continent, legal practitioners can be found using, abandoning, bending, sidestepping, replacing and reinterpreting the law (1978, p. 4). In addition to socio-cultural-political values, the implementation of the law is further influenced by different categories of identity – sex, gender, race, ethnicity, religion and class – represented among individual legal practitioners and court users. In other words, " ... the ways in which race or gender have been constructed in society at large [are] inseparable from the rules of evidence or the presumptions at work in ... courthouses" (Rosen, 2008, p. 65). Yet, the influence of different perspectives, experiences and identities are not, in and of themselves, problematic. Justices L'Heureux-Dubé and McLachlin noted in Canadian Supreme Court case RDS v R:

> ... the test for reasonable apprehension of bias established in jurisprudence is reflective of the reality that while judges can never be neutral, in the sense of purely objective, they can and must strive for impartiality. It therefore recognizes as inevitable and appropriate that the differing experiences of judges assist them in their process and will be reflected in their judgments, so long as those experiences are relevant to the cases, are not based on inappropriate stereotypes, and do not prevent a fair and just determination of the cases based on the facts in evidence. (Graycar, 2008, p. 76)

Still, impartiality and fairness require awareness and acknowledgement of subjective influence.

> True impartiality does not require that the judge have no sympathies or opinions; it requires that the judge nevertheless be free to entertain and act upon different points of view with an open mind. (Graycar, 2008, p. 76)

A significant body of empirical research that has developed over the last two decades on the topic of implicit bias has given further credence to the notion that individual legal practitioners affect the implementation of the law. Implicit bias refers to the automatic and unconscious categorization of people and events resulting in a mental attitude that may not be recognized by the person expressing it. This implicit categorization is based on direct experiences as well as the influence of media, culture, religion, politics, language and so on; and can be reflected in assumptions of a specific stereotype and in an overall negative or positive evaluation of a group or individual (Kang, 2009). Implicit bias has been found to impact legal decision-making processes ranging from police intervention to the sentencing choices of judges (Kang *et al.*, 2012). For example, a number of researchers have identified the existence of an implicit gender bias among legal professionals (both men and women) in the US that identifies women as either "workplace cutthroats or, conversely ... secretaries or housewives" (Levinson & Young, 2010, p. 2).

Still, even in the US, where research on implicit bias spans two decades, legal practitioners are slow to accept the role or possibility of bias, implicit or explicit, in their work. Hilarie Bass, Chair of the American Bar Association Litigation Section noted in 2011:

> ... if anyone were to suggest, even politely, that lawyers were as biased as anyone else, few in our profession would not instinctively take umbrage. Indeed, we fashion ourselves the very stewards of equality in our society; the leaders charged with eradicating discrimination. (The Neuroscience of Implicit Bias)

Legal professionals from Bosnia and Herzegovina also strongly adhere to the belief that they apply the law in a strictly objective and impartial manner. Commonly, responses to questions related to the subjectivity of legal deliberation include the refrain that they simply 'apply the legal code'. This attitude is partly attributable to the specific legal framework in the country. Until 2003, Bosnia and Herzegovina employed a comprehensive civil law approach. Even though significant elements of the common law system have been introduced into criminal procedures, influenced by the ICTY and other international agents, judges and legal professionals are still trained mainly in civil law practices (DeNicola, 2010). The fact that the civil law system is highly codified intensifies the notion among judges that they are simply implementing laws that are designed to guard against subjectivity. In other words, legal professionals in Bosnia and Herzegovina generally express the opinion that legal decision making is a simple matter of establishing facts and applying appropriate laws, which are inherently objective.

It is against this backdrop that research on the influence of gender within the judiciary of Bosnia and Herzegovina was undertaken. This research represents one part of a larger, multi-year development project on gender and judicial reform in BiH that is still ongoing, which aims to increase the capacities of judges and prosecutors to integrate gender awareness into the procedures and practices of the BiH judiciary and thereby strengthen the ability of judicial professionals to deliver non-discriminatory services.

Methods

This research served as an initial inquiry into the opinions, attitudes and experiences of a diverse sample of legal professionals working within the BiH judiciary. As such, quantitative and qualitative data collection methods were used, including an anonymous online questionnaire and semi-structured in-person interviews. All questionnaire data were self-reported and, since the aim was to uncover gender-related attitudes within the judiciary, were not validated against empirical evidence (court cases, statistics, etc.). In other words, the data were not treated as a statistically significant representation of substantive legal outcomes of the judiciary, but rather served to provide insights and analysis into the gender-related opinions, beliefs and biases of members of the BiH judiciary.

The researchers designed the questionnaire to capture quantifiable data as well as qualitative narrative responses. Questions allowed respondents to choose one or several answers from a set of choices as well as provide examples for further explanation. In total, 131 online questionnaires were completed by 42 judges, 21 prosecutors, nine lawyers, 21 court associates, three respondents who identified themselves as 'other', and 35 individuals who did not disclose information about their professional status. Of 96 respondents, 52% identified themselves as male and 48% identified themselves as female.

In addition to questionnaires, data were also collected using semi-structured interviews, which are suitable for exploring people's experiences, values and attitudes in some depth, and are used for researching sensitive topics (Byrne, 2006). The interviews were loosely based on the same questions posed in the survey, but were asked in a different way, allowing for open-ended responses and the natural evolution of discussion. This strategy brought forth some crucial issues that were not identified through questionnaires.

The research relied extensively on a purposive sampling strategy, whereby the researcher, on the basis of informed judgement, makes a deliberate attempt to select cases or individuals that are representative of the population (Gobo, 2004). A total of 30 in-person interviews were conducted with seven prosecutors, 14 judges and nine attorneys from across BiH. Interviewees included judges from first and second instance courts and prosecutors from cantonal and district prosecutors' offices. The researchers tried to target a mix of male and female interviewees of varying ages, with various legal backgrounds, and from both the criminal and civil-legal sectors.

Concerns about confidentiality and anonymity proved to be a major challenge in data collection. The researchers attributed this to the scrutiny the judicial profession is currently under in BiH society. This could be the reason why a number of potential respondents refused to fill out the questionnaire, and why some respondents skipped questions about their professional status.

While 161 total responses were collected, including both online questionnaires and in-person interviews, it is possible that some interviewees also completed the questionnaire and therefore the exact number of individual respondents is not known.

Due to the sensitive nature of this research, and to minimize prejudicing the answers of respondents and interviewees, questions never directly used either the word 'gender' or the word 'influence'. In addition, the questionnaire and interview tools avoided the use of 'value language' that denoted either a negative or positive attitude about the topics of inquiry. Thus, terms such as 'gender bias', 'discrimination', 'differential treatment' and 'harassment' were avoided except in the case of 'sexual harassment', which was used only in questions asked in relation to the existence of policies and in-house training programmes.

Findings: gendered variation in attitudes concerning the representation of women judges

Women in Bosnia and Herzegovina hold approximately 60% of all judicial posts (HJPC, 2012). While a number of studies have examined the representation of women in judicial positions in some countries compared to others (Remiche, 2013; Schultz & Shaw, 2013), this research was concerned with the explanations offered by legal professionals in BiH for the relatively high rate of representation of women within the BiH judiciary. And indeed, stereotypes and gendered attitudes were present in the responses of both women and men on this topic.

Responses were notably differentiated by the gender of the respondent. Women tended to hold a positive view of the role of judges and, in particular, the work of women judges, while men tended to minimize the role of judges and, by association, women's capabilities as judges. For example, a female judge framed the gender balance of judges in the following way:

> There are more women [in judicial positions] because this is a very hard job with a large caseload and women are harder working and more responsible than men. Men tend to stay away from the position of judge because this job is no longer very valued and is not properly rewarded.

This sentiment was consistent with another female judge who remarked that "... court is work with a large case load that needs to be dealt with, and women are more dedicated in that way". A female lawyer reiterated this belief when she asserted, "... women are more dedicated to their jobs".

In contrast, a male judge postulated that the job of judge is attractive to women because it is not strenuous. He remarked:

> The judiciary is a predominantly female job because it is easier – a sitting job which does not require physical effort.... There are now more male lawyers, but women are slowly occupying that sphere too.

Perhaps even more interesting, one male prosecutor went so far as to link the gendered nature of power relations between women and men in the home to the representation of women in the BiH judiciary. He postulated:

> Maybe because women are subordinate to men at home they apply for judicial positions; because in this position they are dominant at work, which compensates for their situation at home.

In addition, two of the 131 responses to the online survey included voluntary narrative comments from respondents who both identified themselves as male judges, indicating their belief that a "gender imbalance" in the BiH judiciary was "interfering with their work". Presumably, these two judges were referring to the slight majority women have in judicial appointments. It is unclear precisely how these two male judges see women's representation as 'interfering' with judicial work, but Professor of Law Reg Graycar from the University of Sydney has argued that women and minority judges are subject to particular scrutiny for 'bias' by their white, male counterparts (2008).

These responses provide examples of gender stereotyping by both women and men in the judiciary. Women distinguish themselves as better suited for legal positions in relation to their 'natural' characteristic of being harder working and more responsible than men; and by contrast suggest that men are less hard working and responsible. Men characterize women as innately less capable (by describing the job itself as not difficult) or motivated by a desire for power and domination (in contrast to an interest in the law or justice).

While this handful of responses does not provide definitive evidence that the BiH judiciary is compromised by discriminatory gender stereotypes, these findings do suggest that legal professionals hold explicit gender-based attitudes. The extent to which these attitudes might also operate at the implicit level is unclear; but a substantial body of research from North America suggests that implicit biases tend to be consistent with prevailing socio-cultural hierarchies (Kang, 2009, p. 3).

Findings: collegial relationships and courthouse atmosphere

Respectful and fair treatment among and between judges, prosecutors, attorneys and other court professionals is arguably an indicator of the level of awareness these professionals bring to bias and therefore of their ability to implement the law impartially. This research revealed that collegial relationships and courthouse atmospheres in BiH are not always strictly professional and formal, despite assertions from the vast majority of respondents that they are. The findings illustrate that women in particular may still suffer from biased treatment in the work place, even when they have risen to the position of judge.

For example, in the online questionnaire, 24% of respondents (or 31 out of 127) reported either witnessing or personally experiencing a member of the judiciary being called or referred to by a name other than their title or surname in the courtroom or courthouse – including diminutives and endearments such as 'honey', 'sweetie' and 'girl'. These data were reinforced by a number of anecdotes shared during interviews. One female attorney recounted being called 'girl' in court by a male attorney, behaviour she interpreted as an attempt to discredit her. Another female, a judge, recalled a male judge turning to her during a courtroom proceeding and asking, "What did you want to say, beautiful?".

Early research from the US concluded that terms of endearment or comments on appearance that call attention to an individual as a woman, rather than as a judicial professional, can significantly undercut her credibility and perceived professionalism (Eich, 1985, p. 340). Further, formal titles denote a superordinate position while familiar terms, even under the pretext of a compliment, denote a subordinate role (Levine, 1987, p. 780). This can give the appearance of favour to one legal professional over another and thereby call into question the impartiality of proceedings.

Results of the online questionnaire also indicated that 28% of respondents (36 out of 127) had either witnessed or been the subject of jokes about women, including references to sexual attractiveness or the lack thereof, as well as 'dumb blonde' jokes. Jokes about women made up the single greatest category of jokes reported by judicial professionals, though jokes made about men were a relatively close second – with 22% of respondents (29 out of 127) reporting having witnessed or been the subject of them. While the majority of respondents (62%) reported that they had neither witnessed nor experienced jokes made about women, men, race, ethnicity, national identity, socio-economic status, physical appearance, age or other topics, it is notable that the two single largest categories of jokes are specifically gender related. This is further evidence of gender-based stereotypes at work within the BiH courts.

Sexual and gender-based harassment can also contribute to uncomfortable or hostile working conditions. Yet all interviewees reported that they were not aware of in-house policies on sexual harassment nor had they been to in-house trainings on the subject. These data were also supported by questionnaire data, which revealed that 34% of respondents were not aware of the sexual harassment policies or laws that govern the court and 24% did not know whether any such policies or laws exist. And, while there are 'Rule Books' that govern the courthouse workplace and codes of ethics for judges and prosecutors, the issue of sexual or gender-based harassment is not explicitly addressed.

One prosecutor reported in an interview that he believes sexual harassment does exist within the judiciary, but that very little effort is made to create awareness and understanding. He made the following remark:

> In staff meetings we do not talk about sexual harassment and discrimination and there is no awareness of it. It is very hard to distinguish what is sexual harassment. I think it happens everywhere. For example, we say things jokingly that we actually think [are true].

There were a number of interviewees who trivialized the problem of sexual harassment and questioned the need for a policy at all. Yet, several others shared observations or anecdotes which could be considered to describe sexual harassment. For example, one male attorney mentioned that his colleague told a prosecutor that "he has a problem when she is there because he has sexual fantasies about her". Similarly, another male attorney at a different courthouse suggested that his colleagues will sometimes openly (within the hearing of others) express interest in sexual relations with women working within the judiciary.

While these cases may not be representative, in combination with reflections from interviewees that a sexual harassment policy is *not* necessary and questionnaire data showing that sex or gender-based jokes are not uncommon, these examples of inappropriate comments signal the need for a concerted awareness and prevention effort. In other words, a lack of in-house policies on sexual harassment and of familiarity with what constitutes sexual harassment are creating an environment of ambiguity in which harassment and inappropriate behaviour can and do occur within BiH courts. This environment can have negative consequences for those working in the courts, as well as for judicial decision making and substantive legal outcomes.

Indeed, openly negative or sexualized attitudes toward women can directly affect their credibility; their own sense of credibility as well as perceptions of credibility by colleagues, clients, litigants and witnesses. Most notably, this can result in a *de facto* court environment that lacks impartiality and fairness. Moreover, a professional atmosphere where gender-based stereotypes are sometimes the basis for jokes can create an unpleasant or even hostile working environment for individuals and groups and may also constitute a form of sexual harassment. And while respondents did not volunteer examples of the types of jokes made about men, and the research therefore did not identify whether they are of a gendered nature (or pejorative), international research has revealed that men also report feeling harassed – by women and men – particularly in situations where they believe they are being mocked for not living up to "... traditional heterosexual male gender role[s]" (Waldo *et al.*, 1998, p. 61).

While the topic of sexual harassment is complicated and sensitive, it is a documented workplace reality around the world (Fiedler & Blanco, 2006). Sexual harassment is deeply intertwined with gender stereotypes and attitudes, the real and perceived differences between women and men, and the expectations and assumptions assigned to them based on their gender. Sexual harassment in any form can contribute to uncomfortable, unfair, and discriminatory working conditions. Moreover, by treating individuals or groups differently, sexual and gender-based harassment can effectively contribute to a lack of impartiality – whether perceived or factual.

Findings: gender and decision making on child custody

Substantive legal outcomes represent perhaps the most significant area of concern with regard to the issue of gender bias. This research (Halilović & Huhtanen, 2014) examined the views and attitudes of judges, attorneys, prosecutors and court associates on a number of substantive legal issues ranging from child custody, domestic and sexual violence, credibility of witnesses and victims, and views on inheritance. This article will focus on the findings related to child custody.

If gender-based stereotypes and attitudes directly influence legal decision making and judicial outcomes, then the aim of impartial and non-discriminatory justice is compromised. Previous literature by practitioners and scholars of the law has linked rigid gender stereotypes that are associated with parenting to decision making in child custody cases. Lynn Hecht Schafran, Director of the National Judicial Education Program in the US for over 20 years, has asserted that:

> Many judges, domestic relations commissioners, family services officers, and custody evaluators have an underlying sense that women belong in the domestic sphere of the home, providing care to young and old, whereas men belong in the public sphere of the paid work world, bringing home the bacon, but never cooking it. (1994, p. 26)

In other words, men can be confronted with stereotypes that cause court professionals to assume they are simply not as capable or appropriate as women in the role of primary caregiver. This may have little to do with their actual interest, ability or experience in parenting. Thus, if gender-based stereotypes serve as a basis for judicial decision making, a problematic, if not discriminatory, framework for the resolution of child custody cases may result.

This research also revealed the existence of rigid gender-based stereotypes and attitudes among members of the BiH judiciary in relation to child rearing and child custody. Among 30 interviewees, all but four indicated that they believe placing children with the mother is the best practice. Judges, lawyers and defence counsel alike asserted that entrusting children to the mother is fair and constitutes the most favourable solution for children. Interviewees consistently reported that this preference is due to the natural connection between a mother and child. Additional explanations represented variations on this theme, including:

- there is a strong bond between a mother and a child;
- mothers are natural caregivers; and
- mothers take better care of children.

Interviewees felt these factors were especially pertinent in cases where the children were five years or younger. They rated the type of housing available to the mother, the type of work the parents do, and the financial situation of each parent less relevant than keeping the children with the mother. One female judge, who cited the "natural connection" between mothers and their children, did indicate that the option of awarding custody to fathers is considered in some cases. She made the following remark:

> When children are small, the opinion is that there is a natural connection between a child and its mother. However, it depends a lot on the concrete situation, because I know many situations when a child is entrusted to the father. It is not so rare, but more often a child is entrusted to its mother because of the natural connection.

Yet, this comment still reflects the belief that mothers share a connection with their children that fathers do not. And despite the assertion of this judge that children are entrusted to the father in "many situations", the research findings suggest that women constitute the presumptive best choice for primary caregiver even, in some cases, in contravention to the 'best interests of the child', the legal standard in BiH. Remarkably, one lawyer was under the impression that BiH law actually stipulates that custody of children be awarded to the mother – which is factually incorrect. This illustrates how gender-based stereotypes and attitudes can be so strong that they override legal reality.

Online questionnaire responses were consistent with those of interviewees, indicating that 70% of respondents believe that whether the parent is the mother is an important factor in making a decision about child custody. Interestingly, women and men answered this question without gender differentiation. These findings suggest that BiH court professionals favour mothers over fathers in child custody cases due to explicit gender biases and irrespective of the facts of the case. In addition, a number of interviews further revealed, anecdotally, that fathers in BiH may not petition for custody at all, due to their perception that the judiciary will automatically award children to the mother.

While men may be faced with stereotypes that lead court professionals to assume they are not as capable or appropriate as women in the role of primary caregiver, the reality is that the majority of child care providers in familial settings are women. This is also a factor in why mothers are awarded primary custody in so many cases – they have a greater demonstrated commitment to child rearing (Cadwell, 1993, p. 222). Thus, the issue as far as the judiciary is concerned is not necessarily whether women are awarded custody more often than men, but whether presumptive gender-based stereotypes play a role in judicial decision making. Indeed, it may be true in BiH, as it is elsewhere, that women do spend more time raising and caring for children and families. Yet in cases in which the father has taken up an active role in parenting and has an interest in primary custody, it would be discriminatory for members of the judiciary to assume that he is not capable solely on the basis of his gender.

Discussion

The gender-based stereotypes and attitudes revealed through both the online questionnaire and in-person interviews were explicit, for respondents openly provided their opinions. Still, expressing explicit gender-based biases may be different from being aware that these beliefs constitute such biases. If stereotypes and attitudes are not challenged in a social context, people are more likely to express them freely; but if biases are seen as unfavourable in a social context, people generally try to hide them (Kang *et al.*, 2012). It remains unclear whether any of the respondents in this research would identify or recognize their comments as explicitly gender biased. However, insights can be derived from research conducted throughout the European Union (EU) that tested understandings of the concept of gender. Sandy Ruxton and Nikki van der Gaag conducted 70 interviews across 23 EU member states in 2011 and largely found that gender is not a well understood concept. For example, they spoke with Jivka Marinova, Director of the Gender Education, Research and Technologies foundation in Bulgaria, who noted:

> Gender equality has been introduced as a term in public discourse, but it is still an empty term, not well and properly understood by either women or men. When the terms 'gender' and 'gender equality' were introduced they sounded completely alien. Outside of women's NGOs, gender organizations, and some academic circles, they still sound alien. (2013, p. 169)

Moreover, researchers for this study, who have been working with judges, court associates and other legal practitioners in BiH for almost three years, can attest to the limited understanding of the concept of gender among these professionals. Thus, it is plausible that members of the judiciary in BiH may associate gender-based constructions such as social characteristics, behaviours, roles and responsibilities with what they see as biologically-derived and innate qualities of women and men. In this context, explicitly held gender-based stereotypes and attitudes would not be seen as such, but as factual assessments of the differences between the sexes.

Notably, international research has increasingly revealed the limits to which an individual is able to be impartial and objective, regardless of their profession (Greenwald *et al.*, 2009).[1] For example, studies examining the influence of subconscious attitudes, assumptions and stereotypes on decision making have determined that nearly every aspect of behaviour, from how we relate to people who are different from us to how we make choices about the products we buy, are influenced by implicit bias (Kang *et al.*, 2012, pp. 1135–1152). The development of implicit bias begins early in life, when children learn from family, friends and other social influences "to ascribe certain characteristics to members of distinct ethnic and social groups" (Levinson & Young, 2010, p. 6). With age these stereotypes become more ingrained such that even if a person develops an explicit (consciously adopted) non-biased view of the world, "their stereotypes remain largely unchanged and become implicit (or automatic)" (Levinson & Young, 2010, p. 6).[2]

While this research did not seek to assess the influence of implicit biases on the judiciary, it may nonetheless be reflected in the views and attitudes expressed by respondents. Lynn Hecht Schafran, a US legal practitioner who has been researching gender bias in the courts since the mid-1980s, has argued that "stereotypical thinking about the nature and roles of women and men" among legal professionals is one of the most prominent ways in which gender bias influences court operations, procedures, and decision making (1993, p. 397). More recent development of the understanding of implicit bias indicates that this stereotypical thinking can be reflected in both implicit and explicit ways.

This research did identify a number of ways in which explicit gender-related stereotypes and attitudes shape the opinions and beliefs of legal–judicial professionals in BiH. Most notably, the opinions of judges and prosecutors concerning the representation of women on the bench illustrate explicit attitudes concerning the abilities and motivations of women and men. Research findings also suggest that collegial relationships and the court atmosphere are shaped by gender-based stereotypes and attitudes. References to female legal–judicial colleagues that highlight their appearance, or expressions of sexual interest in a female colleague in the courtroom, are evidence of the differential treatment of women in the workplace. And, explicit gender-based attitudes among court professionals in cases of child custody represent a significant impact of gender-based stereotyping as it directly relates to the influence of gender on the implementation of the law.

The focus of this research was to identify explicit bias in the BiH judiciary, but legal professionals and members of the judiciary should be aware of not only their conscious attitudes and views on gender, but the full range of implicit gender-based stereotypes and attitudes they are likely to have assimilated from existing social hierarchies and cultural norms. Therefore, comprehensive steps to uncover, identify and overcome bias – whether explicit or implicit – are critical to upholding the mandate of the judiciary to dispense justice in an impartial and fair manner.

Conclusion

This research illustrates that judicial practice is not necessarily as devoid of socio-cultural influence as some in the BiH judiciary report it to be. Despite the fact that women hold a slight majority in judicial appointments – a feminization of the profession that could be seen as a balancing mechanism for gender-based discrimination – it is clear that gender-based stereotypes persist. Moreover, gender-based stereotypes and attitudes impact the judiciary at all levels of interaction, between and among court professionals, between court professionals and users, and also between court professionals and the law itself, in some cases affecting legal processes and decision making.

Members of the judiciary are faced with the difficult task of exercising legal impartiality despite emotions, beliefs and values that reflect their socio-cultural environment. Nonetheless, democratic judicial institutions consistently espouse their commitment to the principles of fairness and objectivity; and checks and balances, such as judicial panels, appeal courts and jury trials, are regular features of judicial systems. Committed judicial institutions should also promote, if not insist on, training and awareness efforts intended to address the influence of both explicit and implicit gender-based stereotypes and attitudes. Indeed, ensuring judicial impartiality and fairness requires confronting the reality that conscious views and prejudices as well as automatic and subconscious stereotypes and attitudes can and do affect the administration of justice.

Acknowledgements

On behalf of DCAF and the Atlantic Initiative, the authors would like to thank the Norwegian Ministry of Foreign Affairs for funding a multi-year development project on gender and judicial reform in BiH. The research presented in this article was conducted and funded within this project. The authors are also grateful to the High Judicial and Prosecutorial Council of Bosnia and Herzegovina for endorsing and supporting this research and to all the judges, prosecutors, attorneys and court associates who participated in online questionnaires and individual interviews. Finally, the authors would like to thank Kimberly Storr and Callum Watson for their editorial assistance.

Disclosure statement

No potential conflict of interest was reported by the authors.

Notes

[1] A meta-analysis of 122 research reports, involving a total of 14,900 subjects, revealed that implicit bias test (IAT) scores where stereotyping and prejudice are identified better predict behaviour than self-reports.

[2] Also see: Wilson *et al.* (2000), and in particular p. 104.

References

Byrne, B. (2006) Qualitative interviewing, in: C. Seale (Ed) *Researching Society and Culture* (London, SAGE Publications), pp. 206–226.

Cadwell, L.A. (1993) Gender bias against fathers in custody? The important differences between outcome and process, *Vermont Law Review*, 18(1), pp. 215–249.

DeNicola, C.P. (2010) Criminal procedure reform in Bosnia and Herzegovina: between organic minimalism and extrinsic maximalism, pp. 10–12, 64–65, ExpressO. Available at: http://works.bepress.com/christopher_denicola/1, accessed 1 June 2015.

Eich, W. (1985) Gender bias in the courtroom: some participants are more equal than others, *Judicature*, 69, 339–343.

Falk Moore, S. (1978) *Law as Process: An Anthropological Approach* (London, Routledge & Kegan Paul).

Fiedler, A.M. & Blanco, R.I. (2006) The challenge of varying perceptions of sexual harassment: an international study, *Journal of Behavioral & Applied Management*, 7(3), pp. 274–291.

Gobo, G. (2004) Sampling, representativeness and generalizability, in: C. Seale, G. Gobo, J.F. Gubrium, & D. Silverman (Eds) *Qualitative Research Practice* (London, SAGE Publications), pp. 405–426.

Graycar, R. (2008) Gender, race, bias and perspective: OR, how otherness colours your judgement, *International Journal of the Legal Profession*, 15(1–2), pp. 73–86.

Greenwald, A.G., *et al.* (2009) Understanding and using the implicit association test: III. Meta-analysis of predictive validity, *Journal of Personality and Social Psychology*, 97(17), pp. 17–41.

Halilović, M. & Huhtanen, H. (2014) *Gender and the judiciary: the implications of gender within the judiciary of Bosnia and Herzegovina* (Geneva, DCAF).

Hecht Schafran, L. (1993) Is the law male? Let me count the ways, *Chicago-Kent Law Review*, 69(2), pp. 397–411.

Hecht Schafran, L. (1994) Gender bias in family courts: why prejudice permeates the process, *Family Advocate*, 17(1), pp. 22–28.

High Judicial and Prosecutorial Council of Bosnia and Herzegovina (HJPC). (2012) *2012 Annual Report* (Sarajevo).

Kang, J. (2009) *Implicit Bias: A Primer for Courts* (National Center for State Courts, Race and Ethnic Fairness in the Courts).

Kang, J., Bennett, M., Carbado, D., Casey, P., Dasgupta, N., Faigman, D., Godsil, R., Greenwald, A.G., Levinson, J. & Mnookin, J. (2012) Implicit bias in the courtroom, *UCLA Law Review*, 59(5), pp. 1124–86.

Levine, J.A. (1987) Preventing gender bias in the courts: a question of judicial ethics, *Georgetown Journal of Legal Ethics*, 1, p. 780.

Levinson, J.D. & Young, D. (2010) Implicit gender bias in the legal profession: an empirical study, *Duke Journal of Gender Law & Policy*, 18(1), pp. 1–44.

Merry, S.E. (1986) Everyday understandings of the law in working-class America, *American Ethnologist*, 13(2), pp. 253–270.

Remiche, A. (2013) General Introduction to the International Symposium *The Judge Is a Woman*, Brussels, 7–8 November. Available at: http://droit-public.ulb.ac.be/wp-content/uploads/2013/11/02.-Introduction-par-MAD.-REMICHE.mp3.

Rosen, L. (2008) *Law as Culture: An Invitation* (Princeton, NJ, Princeton University Press).

Ruxton, S. & van der Gaag, N. (2013) Men's involvement in gender equality – European perspectives, *Gender and Development*, 21(1), pp. 161–175.

Schultz, U. & Shaw, G. (2013) *Gender and Judging, Oñati International Series in Law and Society* (Portland, OR, Hart Publishing), pp. 9–13.

Shehada, N.Y. (2005) *Justice without Drama: Enacting Family Law in Gaza City Sharīa Court* (Maastricht, Shaker Publishing).

The Neuroscience of Implicit Bias. (2011) Video, American Bar Association Section of Litigation, 6 December, Available at: http://youtu.be/kzz5Ae-Jq0s, viewed 22 June 2014.

Waldo, C.R., Berdahl, J.L. & Fitzgerald, L.F. (1998) Are men sexually harassed? If so, by whom? *Law and Human Behavior*, 22(1), pp. 59–79.

Wilson, T.D., Lindsey, S. & Schooler, T.Y. (2000) A Model of Dual Attitudes, *Psychological Review*, 107(1), 101–126.

Gender training for the judiciary in Argentina

BEATRIZ KOHEN
Law School, University of Palermo, Buenos Aires, Argentina

ABSTRACT *In this paper I describe the two major Argentine experiences of gender training for the judiciary against the background of two relevant trends, women's entry in considerable numbers into the judiciary and the process of expansion of women's rights initiated after the restoration of democracy. The gap between the passing of progressive legislation and its lack of enforcement speaks of a tradition of women's subordination that is much engrained in our society and in its legal system. In spite of the existence of progressive egalitarian legislation stereotyped thinking prevails to prevent progressive legal practices. This constitutes a strong argument for gender training of the judiciary. I will argue that, although separated in time, and different in scope, the initiatives share common objectives and there is a strong connection between them, clearly identifiable in the processes developed by some of its main characters. The coverage of the Asociación de Mujeres Juezas de Argentina (AMJA) project was limited to a small number of its members. Differently, the OFICINA DE LA MUJER (OM) experience aims to train the whole of the judiciary – judges, judicial staff and administrative employees. The paper discusses the tensions underlying each of the programmes and the risks of backlash. It advocates for the development of phenomenological, slower and more continuous gender trainings, attentive to subjectivity and the promotion of identity transformations. It also supports impact evaluation as a means to ascertain the effects of gender education on the judiciary as an institution and on judges' everyday work and decisions that will allow establishing its relevance, correcting its shortcomings and thus ensuring its legitimacy and continuity.*

> As a rule our judicial powers have not been very progressive. We need to fight prejudices that many pretend to be traditions.[1] (Justice Carmen Argibay)

The Argentine context for gender training for the judiciary

After the restoration of democracy in the early 1980s, a movement towards reform took hold of the Argentine judiciary amidst expanding economic globalization and privatization. Instilled by international cooperation banks, judicial reform sought to introduce the mechanisms that would ensure judicial security allowing for international investment to flourish; more notably, contemporary technology, modern managerial and computing skills, alternative methods of dispute resolution, a more transparent method for the appointment of judges, the shift from an adversarial to an inquisitorial criminal system and improved access to the justice system. Judicial reform is also associated with democratic consolidation, governance and enforcement of human, social and economic rights (Garro, 2004).

While in other jurisdictions judicial reform has had a gender mainstreaming component, in the Argentine case, until very recently, attempts to reform the judiciary did not consider gender at all, even less promote gender mainstreaming. Thus, it is often argued that feminists arrived too late to influence judicial reform.

At the same time, the recovery of democracy in Argentina (1983) and the Constitutional Reform (1994) were milestones in the expansion of women's rights. The International Convention for the Elimination of All Forms of Discrimination against Women (CEDAW) was signed by Argentina in 1980 and gained legal standing in 1985, although the Optional Protocol was not ratified until 2006. In 1996, Argentina signed the Inter-American Convention to Punish, Prevent and Eradicate All Forms of Violence against Women (Belém do Pará). Both conventions, later ratified by the state, became legally binding and served as a framework for the passing of new legislation on gender discrimination and gender violence compelling the state to implement public policies aimed at attaining gender equality. As a consequence, over the last thirty years, Argentina has made significant progress in terms of the enactment of local legislation aimed at ensuring the integration of women into economic, political and social development in equal terms with men. Particular attention has been paid to establishing equality for women as a constitutional right, eliminating discriminatory measures, passing special laws to deal with specific problems, and creating and strengthening women's advocacy units at national, provincial and municipal levels. As a result, women have gained legal equality in the letter of the law, but this has not been fully translated into practice. Important gaps persist. In the 1980s and 1990s feminist advocacy concentrated on changing legislation. However, the problem in Argentina seems to be one of enforcement rather than one related to the existence of specific legislation. A traditional context of strong sexism and gender discrimination leaves gender matters at the very bottom of the political agenda; resistance prevents legal implementation. Thus, more recently, as the rights strategy proved elusive, the women's movement has started to demand substantive gender equality, pointing to the judiciary as a potential ally in its quest for gender justice.

With this in mind, the 1992 General Recommendation n°19 of the CEDAW Committee declares as indispensable the training of judicial officers, security forces and other social officials for the application of the CEDAW convention. Similarly, documents signed by the Supreme Court of the Nation (SCN) at various Latin American Supreme Court Magistrate's summits prescribe gender mainstreaming (Cancún Declaration, 2002[2] and 'Brasilia rules for Access to Justice', 2008[3]).

As already mentioned, the Belem do Pará Convention and the new Law on Gender-based Violence (Law 26485/09) lay down an extensive programme that calls for the articulation of the three powers of the nation, inviting all government sectors to struggle against the multiple forms of gender-based violence (physical, sexual, psychological, economic, social, institutional, by the media . . .). The judiciary constitutes one among the many significant collective actors that should join in this struggle against gender discrimination and gender violence by becoming more aware of gender stereotyping in the process of law enforcement and interpretation.

As judges make decisions that strongly affect people's lives, they have the power to contribute to transforming gender relations and promoting gender equality, both within the confines of the judiciary, and within society at large. The mere possibility for the judges to reflect upon the ways gender impinges on the administration of justice will probably generate changes in their world vision with the capacity to influence their decisions and impact on the lives of those involved in legal conflicts. However, frequently they know little about gender. This is not surprising as the law curriculum in our universities does not include any compulsory course on gender, which entails that most law graduates have never received any instruction on gender. The same applies to judges.[4]

In spite of the growing prestige of gender issues within the social sciences, there is strong resistance to gender mainstreaming in legal academia. Actually, law schools are considered amongst the most conservative sectors of academia, its gender blindness promotes gender stereotyping, hinders judges' as well as other legal operators' understanding of women's needs and realities with the result of obstructing women's access to justice. As members of our culture, judges are socialized into accepting the prevailing gender stereotypes, prejudices, norms and values legitimating women's subordination.

Anyhow, it is only very recently that gender has acquired any significance for the judges' activity. Even when the judges believe certain gender-based legal problems to be serious, they often do not understand how gender impinges on women's lives and their relation to the law. Furthermore, sometimes they are not familiar with gender relevant international human rights conventions or local legislation, or with ways of using these to benefit women.

The need for effective gender training of the judiciary is certainly there. Such an education might accelerate cultural change enabling a just and equal treatment for men and women who come to the courts in search of solutions to their legal problems and of fair decisions taking into account the specificities of women's gendered lives.

Gender training for the judiciary in Argentina

Two main gender training programmes for the judiciary stand out in Argentina: the 'Towards a Jurisprudence of Equality Programme' (1997–2000) and the current 'Plan to Introduce Gender Mainstreaming in the Argentine Judiciary' (started in 2010). The charismatic leadership of Justice Argibay, recently deceased, has been behind the start, execution and success of both experiences.

In the past, other attempts have been few, very fragmentary and isolated. Presently, there are some embryonic initiatives in different sections of the judiciary where gender or women's offices are being created.

The 'Towards a Jurisprudence of Equality' (JEP) programme was carried out between 1997 and 2000 by the Argentine Association of Women Judges (AMJA), in partnership with the International Association of Women Judges (IAWJ) and funded by the Inter American Bank. Its main objectives were to introduce a gender perspective in legal analysis with a strong focus on domestic violence, and to promote the application of International Conventions of Human Rights with an emphasis on the Convention to Eliminate All Forms of Discrimination Against Women.

The second programme, the 'Plan to Introduce Gender Mainstreaming in the Argentine Judiciary' started much later, towards the beginning of 2010, triggered by the ratification of the Convention of Belem do Pará and the passing of Law 24685/2009 on Gender-based Violence. It is being developed by the 'Oficina de la Mujer' (Women's Office) of the Supreme Court of the Nation, created in 2009 with a very ambitious target: to offer every judge (both men and women) and every judicial officer and administrative employee of the country's courts some training on gender. Although there is a significant time gap between those programmes, there certainly is a strong connection between them.

The Jurisprudence of Equality Programme

Towards 1997, the Jurisprudence of Equality Programme (JEP) started in Argentina, following Judge Argibay's,[5] earlier connections[6] with the International Association of Women Judges and the subsequent creation of the Argentine Association of Women Judges. The programme provided training for members of the judiciary in the domestic application of international, regional and national law on issues dealing with discrimination and violence against women. Its ultimate goal was to build a true 'jurisprudence of equality' – one based on universal principles of human rights. JEP training workshops and seminars brought judges together to focus on the concrete meaning of abstract guarantees of equal protection and non-discrimination. Through case studies, problem-solving exercises and other adult learning techniques, judges had the opportunity to share insights with colleagues and deepen their understanding of international law as applied to domestic contexts. Using a Train the Trainers (3T)[7] methodology, the programme trained AMJA members to carry out workshops with other judges aimed at alerting them to hidden gender biases and stereotypes and promoting awareness of gender discrimination and gender-based violence.

The training of core trainers in Washington and Buenos Aires on how to prepare interactive seminars and the provision of materials was followed by training seminars held in most Argentine provinces. Sixteen seminars were held covering most Argentine provinces and including 251 judges between 1997 and 2000.

Evaluations of the seminars were performed at the end of each seminar and most participants rated highly both the trainers and the materials used. Training was useful in terms of making members more sensitive to the effects of gender discrimination and gender violence and more aware of the biases involved in their daily work (AMJA). No attempt was made, however, to evaluate the long-term impact of the programme, namely, whether trainees used the international conventions in their judgments or, whether, as a consequence of increased awareness, they had introduced procedural changes to the treatment of cases, or whether they had included gender issues in the content of the courses they taught. The fact that the programme itself did not proceed to evaluate its long-term impact does not mean that it could not have been done retrospectively.

In the meantime, although this is certainly a very rough measure, examining the path followed by the first cohort of judges trained to become replicators of the experience allows us to see that quite a few of these first replicators have risen to high positions within the judiciary and are making a difference both for women who come to court and for women within the system. Two of these women[8] have been judges in the Supreme Court of the Nation. On top of their regular tasks as members of the highest court, both have headed important newly created offices aimed at improving women's life conditions: the (OVD) 'Domestic Violence Office' under the coordination of Justice Helen Highton created in 2005, and the 'Women's Office' (OM) created in 2009 led by Justice Carmen Argibay. Additionally, Dr Stella Maris Martínez, now the head of the Office of the National Defense,[9] has made gender a central issue within her administration. Others are now participating actively in the OM training programme and still others are working to enhance AMJA's activities (Bohmer, 2009). This confirms an early observation by Durham (1998) that women judges' organizations can be powerful forces in initiating and moving forward social transformations.

The Plan to Introduce Gender Mainstreaming in the Argentine Judiciary

Introduction. The gender training strategy for the judiciary recently initiated (2010), the so called 'Plan to Introduce Gender Mainstreaming in the Argentine Judiciary' carried out by the Women's Office of the Supreme Court of the Nation (OM), is much more encompassing than its name suggests, as it purports "it should be considered as a strategy within a wider plan attempting to gender mainstream the judiciary", as established by the 'Acordada 13/2009'.[10] As a matter of fact, the 'Women's Office' (OM) of the SCN was created to foster the incorporation of a gender perspective in the institutional planning and the internal processes of the judiciary to achieve gender equality both for judicial actors and for users of the system.

Apart from gender training – which consists of incorporating the gender perspective in the judiciary and disseminating the principles of the CEDAW and the Belem do Pará international conventions – the design and implementation of training seminars for members of the judiciary, administrative and court staff and its monitoring also involve the construction of a previously missing gender map[11] for the whole of the country. This was crucial to provide an idea of the gender distribution of the judiciary. In fact, this production of a 'gender map' was the first public activity of the OM (2010).

While Law 26.485/09 engaged every power of the nation to assume responsibility in the process of gender mainstreaming, the OM has certainly taken a leadership role, thus providing a model for other branches of government whose activities in this direction have been far less energetic, varying considerably according to the different ministries and even offices within the same ministry.

In the view of the OM, Argentine judges do not apply consistently and across-the-board the international legal instruments signed by the Argentine state aiming to guarantee women's equality. As a consequence, these rights are not being enforced.

The OM has also substantiated instances of discriminatory treatment of women victims as well as judgments that fail to take into account the disadvantages suffered by many women because they live in a 'sexist, patriarchal system'. Legal operators are not trained to be able to detect the various situations in which women are at a disadvantage. There is a need to raise awareness on gender issues and promote the incorporation of a gender perspective among judges, prosecutors, court officers and administrative employees of the justice system so that they become aware of prevailing sexual stereotypes.

The training programme. At this point, I will concentrate on describing the ways the programme is being planned and conducted. It is very important to realize that the programme is being deployed in parallel to this analysis. While a retrospective perspective is not yet possible, it is exciting to follow the project activities as they progress.

The OM programme's target is ambitious, that is to offer gender training to every judge (man and woman) and every judicial officer and administrative employee of the courts. This is consistent with the OM's plan to gender mainstream the judiciary. The idea of gender mainstreaming in general grew out of the failure of specific policies to bring about positive change in women's situation. It is coincident with a global and encompassing attempt to transform gender relations.

The training seminars designed by the OM and validated by the UN combine theoretical and practical components. Their purpose is to cultivate reflection and discussion about the effects of gender stereotyping in judicial decisions. The workshops aim to provide participants with conceptual tools promoting awareness of gender bias in the everyday activity of the courts and to enforce constitutional mandates and international conventions signed by the Argentine state.

In order to cover every jurisdiction in the country, the programme elaborates a basic gender training protocol to be applied to the different actors by specially instructed trainers, selected among judges and judicial staff, using a strongly standardized workshop model and a 3T Train the Trainers methodology.

The programme was publicly launched in the second half of 2010 with the first set of five-day training sessions for core replicators. Although there is a basic common protocol, variations were then introduced to make it more applicable to the diverse settings addressed – highly placed judges, ordinary judges, court staff and administrative staff.

The option to go beyond judges is particularly important in the case of Argentina where, although oral criminal courts were introduced in the 1980s, most of the process is written. This involves an incredible amount of paper work, a lot to be read and written. The only way for the judge to deal with this huge workload is through significant delegation to court staff.

The first core of trainers was selected on the basis of three criteria. Firstly, a higher position in the hierarchy, secondly, teaching experience and, thirdly, previous knowledge of the subject matter. In the first six months the OM trained the first core 200 trainers who would later plan and organize the replicas in each jurisdiction. My impression is that it would not be an exaggeration to say that the programme has an obsessively organized structure catering for all eventualities.

The OM first offered a first five-day seminar for members of the Provincial Supreme Tribunals and Federal High Courts of Second Instance, followed by a five-day seminar for trainers situated in lower positions. Later, they decided to shorten trainers' seminars (to last for three instead of five days). The replicas last one full day.

In 2011, human trafficking for sexual exploitation was added to the curriculum. Thus, a new training protocol on Gender and Trafficking was drawn up in association with a specialized section of the Prosecutor's Office (UFASE) designed for a one-day workshop aimed at sensitizing members of the judiciary and the prosecutor's office.

In the same year, 220 replicators – including 40 members of the security forces – divided over three training seminars were taught to apply the new version of the training protocol in a three-day scheme workshop. In turn, these facilitators are replicating one-day workshops in their own jurisdictions with groups of 30 trainees from among judges, prosecutors and judicial officers.

The estimate of the OM was that by December 2011, 8,000 persons out of a total of 39,254 would have undertaken the gender training, corresponding to 1,554 workshops, exceeding their initial expectation. By the end of April 2012 they had reached 10,000 trainees from every jurisdiction of the country and each section of the judiciary, trained by 250 replicators in 475 sessions. In July 2014, the present director of the OM, in a public address rendering homage to Justice Argibay, referred to a total of "more than 700 replicators carrying out more than 800 workshops reaching almost 30,000 trainees".[12]

In the training workshops, the future facilitators review the tools and instruments offered by the right to equality before the law, women's rights, and the use of non-sexist language, and discuss how to avoid discriminatory terms. They engage in exercises that allow them to reflect on how gender-based social and labour roles are assigned.

The training of future replicators is carried out in Buenos Aires, trainees from other parts of the country have to travel there. Sessions consist of theoretical presentations by gender experts and practical participatory exercises. While trainers were given live theoretical lectures, videos were prepared to be used for the replicas together with instructions on how to proceed with the seminars. Taylor-made for the experience, the materials are very good. Originally, in 2010, there was a manual for each category – judges, court staff and administrative staff, one for trainers and one for attendants. Now there is one for trainers and one for attendants irrespective of their position.[13]

The decision to select trainers from within the judiciary rather than from among gender experts rests on the belief that judges who are a very high-profile group will prefer to be instructed by a peer. In their view, this avoids issues of judges' independence.[14] Last but not least, there is the financial aspect: the judges and other court staff working as replicators do not charge to do it.

The training of the instructors places a strong emphasis on pedagogical, procedural and methodological aspects. During the last day of the training, students practice through role playing, taking turns to teach their colleagues what they were taught the previous two days. The OM's assumption is that the videos cover the theoretical aspects of the training and hence the trainers do not need to be experts in the subject matter. Instead, they need to know very well how to conduct the workshop.

The choice to train such a large contingent certainly creates a tension with the requirements of gender training that do not fit in well with the pressure to train great numbers of people with limited resources. As gender is such an important existential anchor, any attempt to transform gender relations touches upon crucial aspects of human identity, and hence produces strong personal and psychological turmoil. Giving countenance to this commotion would require some expert follow-up, difficult to implement on such a large scale. The present replica model – one all-day of training – does not allow for such a close and sensitive consideration. In my view, the risk that the contents of the course wear out with time should not be underestimated.

Nevertheless, I find the effort valuable since at least a large part of the judicial population, its staff and employees may have some exposure to the issue of gender, a word previously unheard of by most of the persons who will receive the training. Thus, at least the sensitization aspect will be covered.

Ideally, in keeping with gender mainstreaming, the educational system as a whole should be involved in the defeat of gender bias, thus alleviating the pressure on continuous adult education. The curricula at law schools should be intensely scrutinized and provisions made to establish gender and its connections to the law as a valid subject matter within higher legal education.

Obviously, the scope and the magnitude of the project pose a huge challenge for its organizers, more so since the OM works with a very small staff and the government has not made any specific budgetary allocation for its implementation. This means that great demands have been placed on the members of the Women's Office. First, in terms of inciting the Provincial Supreme Tribunals and the Federal Higher Courts to participate in the project by helping to define the needs and demands of the judicial population[15] and selecting the future trainers. The fact that various federal high courts and provincial supreme tribunals have declared the gender training seminar mandatory for all its members should be considered a great achievement. This owes a lot to Justice Argibay's charismatic leadership.

Other challenges successfully addressed have been: (a) to appeal to academics, not belonging to the SCN, who lectured to trainers and recorded their lectures so that the videos could be included in the seminars dictated by the first core of trainers; (b) to ensure the support of local judicial schools that depend on the provincial judicial councils hosting the seminars to providing technical and material support; (c) to raise the funds to design and print the manuals, pay for the expenses involved in the training of the core of instructors, and to recruit core trainers all over the nation to do the job without receiving any payment. More recently, the OM has been trying to effectively respond to the fact that very few highly placed judges have actually attended the workshops, it has associated with the 'Observatorio de Género en la Justicia de la CABA' and elaborated a new seminar model specially formulated to the requirements of high profile judges, working with a different methodology and led by prestigious academics in the legal field.

No doubt the programme has been received extremely well both by the legal community and by the different branches of government and international UN agencies. The OM has been successful in securing financial and logistic support from the top of the judiciary, the provincial Supreme Tribunals and judicial schools, and from various United Nation's agencies providing technical and financial support for the project.

Significantly, in March 2012 the Supreme Court itself decided a very important case addressing a crucial issue on the agenda of women's rights regarding the interpretation of the applicability of 'legal abortion' (art. 86 of the Criminal Code), putting an end to a 100-year controversy. While the conservative prevailing interpretation had restricted the applicability to mentally handicapped rape victims, the Supreme Court understood the clause under discussion as covering every rape victim. This interpretation was in line with the International Treaties subscribed by the Argentine state and the 1994 Reformed Constitution. As explained earlier in this paper, one of the motivations behind the creation of the OM was the need to enforce these new rights for women. This judgment[16] inaugurates a new phase in the ruling of the Supreme Court in an issue such as abortion, so dear to the Argentine women's movement, a renewed institutional culture probably forged by the active role of the OM. Although in Argentina we have a civil law system where precedent does not have the same weight as in common law countries, a Supreme Court judgment is significant in terms of establishing the constitutional interpretation of the Criminal Code. Since in Argentina we do not have a Constitutional Court, the Supreme Court is charged with the interpretation of the constitutionality of law.

Also, other governmental agencies such as the Security Ministry and the National Legislature have asked the OM to provide the same training to their members. Furthermore, in the same spirit, the UN is proposing this protocol as a model for similar initiatives in the rest of Latin America. Most recently, different sessions of the Argentine judiciary have created gender or women's offices that, in turn, are organizing training courses to address their specific needs on the subject.

Parallel and follow-up activities. Neither of the two projects under examination included from the outset an initiative to evaluate whether the training programme actually fulfils its objectives. However, differently from the AMJA project of the 1990s, to compensate for the lack of a more systematic impact evaluation, the OM is organizing various parallel and follow-up activities aimed at assessing the main problems intervening in its implementation and illustrating the relevance of the training to the daily activities of the judiciary.

I call 'parallel activities' those organized by the OM and inspired by the idea to gender mainstream the judiciary but not directly related to the gender training. On the other hand, 'follow-up activities' refer to those related to the training mostly aimed at monitoring the functioning of the training and the training protocol. Many of these activities provide an opportunity to trace the progress of the project.

Parallel activities. As part of this larger plan to gender mainstream the judiciary, the OM has launched various important initiatives: the data collection for the subsequent gender maps of the Argentine judiciary and invitations to all members of the judiciary – irrespective of whether they underwent the training on gender or not – to send judgments related to women's rights and the incorporation of the gender perspective to be disseminated through the OM web page. They have created facilities for lactation and also are starting surveys related to work harassment, work–family balance and care work.

Follow-up activities. The OM requests every trainer to write a report directly after each replica with comments covering difficulties and suggestions raised during the workshop. They also invite every participant to fill in an evaluation form and additionally, as a means to show their commitment to the programme, to make a 'personal contribution to transformation' within a period of two months. The first of these activities is a 'contribution to change' which trainees are expected to send to the OM two months after the training.

In the case of magistrates, this personal contribution can take three forms. The first is writing a paper related to the incorporation of the gender perspective in the judiciary to be published by the SCN. The second option is to send a judgment or decision informed by a gender outlook and produced within a period of two months after the training workshop. The third possibility is to administer a proposed anonymous survey among the judicial staff of the judge's court: participants have to show their level of agreement with a series of traditional statements providing only the sex of the informant. With all these three inputs, the OM prepares its reports.

With a similar purpose OM holds periodic meetings of instructors from all over the country in order to monitor the implementation of the programme. In those meetings facilitators manifest their commitment and enthusiasm for the project, their impression that they are part of some revolutionary transformation, the solidarity that has developed among them and the strengthening of the relationship between the OM and the judiciary. They also identify difficulties and shortcomings and make suggestions. The most frequent criticism relates to funding: the difficulty to raise the funds to cover lunches and coffee breaks and to print the materials for local workshops. In the provinces in which the Supreme Tribunal has not made the replicas mandatory, the instructors also report a certain lack of support and resistance from some higher judges. All this means that the organization of the replicas rests too heavily on the shoulders of the small number of organizers.

The replicators also mention that, at the local level, trainees expect them to be experts on gender issues, facing them with queries well beyond their basic training. Thus they request further gender training for themselves.

It is clear to me that although the recommendations thus gathered may be valuable for future adjustments, these activities cannot replace a systematic assessment of whether the programme actually fulfils its objectives.

As the implementation of programmes aimed at educating the judiciary on gender issues requires the allocation of abundant time, energy and resources, the measurement of its mid and long-term impact is a key element and one particularly valued by funding agencies. Still, while both projects have successfully attempted to measure trainees' satisfaction, through a survey most frequently completed straight after the workshops, the older AMJA project never implemented an evaluation of its long-term impact; nor has the current OM programme as yet made public such an intention.

Particularly in the OM case, the choice not to perform a systematic impact evaluation might relate to the political nature of the endeavour. At the opening of one of the project activities, Justice Argibay expressed her enthusiasm in the following way: "This is like a miracle, an old dream come true, previously unthinkable in the context of such a male-oriented sphere". The OM regards the initiative as a Copernican Revolution, and my impression is that those leading the initiative consider it impossible for the gender training not to produce the desired effect. They also tend to confuse monitoring with impact evaluation.

Because of its youth, any reflection on the challenges and risks the programme might pose is provisional and daring. Although problematic, the inclusion of some activities aimed at measuring its short, mid and long-term effects on the professional visions and procedures of the judiciary and on the legal system as a whole would be recommendable for the future, especially because of its vast scale, but also because of its political nature. As mentioned earlier, the success of the endeavour had a lot to do with Minister Argibay's leadership and charisma, on her view of gender relations and particular understanding of federalism. While her recent death may create a gap that leaves the project prey to a backlash, endangering its continuity, established evaluation results might prove powerful arguments against 'androcentric' resistance or hostility. In her own words with which I began this paper, "one must fight against prejudices".

Disclosure statement

No potential conflict of interest was reported by the author.

Notes

[1] Address by Justice Carmen Argibay in the opening ceremony of the OM , the Women's Office of the National Supreme Court of Justice on September 6, 2010.

[2] The Cancún declaration was issued by the Ibero-American Summit of Supreme Court's Presidents held in the city of Cancún, México on November 27 to 29, 2002.

[3] The Brasilia Regulation for the Access to Justice for vulnerable people have been approved by the XIV Ibero-American Judicial Summit, held in Brasilia on March 4 to 6, 2008. See also the web page of the Women's Office at http://www.csjn.gov.ar/om/trab_unidades/plan_ipgja.pdf

[4] To become a judge in Argentina, one must hold a law degree for a minimum period of five years and compete in a contest organized by the Council of the Judgeship. Although the Councils tend more and more to host schools for the judiciary, there is no compulsory judicial training or a standardized judicial career.

[5] Justice Carmen Argibay was one of the first two women at the Supreme Court of the Nation under a democratic regime. At the time, she was a member of an Oral Criminal Court. She died on 11 May 2014. Elena Highton de Nolasco was the second woman appointed.

[6] For the celebration of its tenth anniversary, the American Association of Women Judges decided to invite women judges from all over the world to a conference held in Washington. The creation of the IAWJ originated at that conference. The idea was supported by 50 women judges from 26 countries including Argentina, represented by Judge Carmen Argibay, from the Criminal Oral Court. The Argentine branch was created in 1993. It has since enjoyed a growing membership and organized various national and international conferences and seminars aided by the financial and technical support of the BID (International World Bank) and the IAWJ. The conferences have addressed basic issues such as Domestic Violence, Child Abuse, Children's Rights and Access to Justice, Women and Marginality, Poverty, Bioethics, the Law and the Female Body. In 2000, the AAWJ (Argentine Association of Women Judges) hosted the biennial International Conference of the IAWJ with a participation of nearly 300 women from all over the world. That year, Judge Argibay was President of the IAWJ.

[7] The 3T methodology, extensively used in training programmes, consists of the implementation of workshops aimed at training future trainers, in this case it was mainly judges who were AMJA members.

[8] See note 2.

[9] This Office provides legal aid to offenders who cannot afford a private lawyer.

[10] See generally the website of the Argentina Supreme Court of the Nation, available at www.csjn.gov.ar.

[11] The gender map presents the gender distribution of the whole of the judicial power, that is to say, every section of the three branches of the judiciary – federal, national and provincial – the Prosecutor's and the General Defender's Office. This involved creating a network with the different jurisdictions that provided the data for each jurisdiction. The map showed that although the judicial power is becoming feminized there is both vertical and horizontal segregation, as women predominate among the administrative and court staff and their presence decreases notably among the judges and more so as one moves to the higher echelons of the judiciary. At the same time women predominate among the first instance civil and labour courts with lesser prestige and their presence decreases when one looks at the federal courts of second instance particularly in the criminal and criminal economic courts. The map can be consulted at the website of the Argentina Supreme Court of the Nation, available at www.csjn.gov.ar.

[12] Dr Flora Acselrad's address in a roundtable on Gender training for the judiciary organised by the UBA Law School in homage to Justice Carmen Argibay.

[13] The manual may be consulted at the website of the Argentina Supreme Court of the Nation website, available at www.csjn.gov.ar.

[14] There is also an urban myth about judges' resistance to receive any training from a social scientist. In fact, Ulrike Schultz observed a similar trend for Germany, and she goes even further to speak about distrust (Schultz 2013, p. 597).

[15] Among the first activities of the OM was a comprehensive consultation with members of the judiciary coming from the provinces held in Buenos Aires in November 2009. In this consultation the need to gender train the judiciary was appraised.

[16] 'F.A.L. s/ medida autosatisfactiva', 13 March 2012.

References

Bohmer, M. Las mujeres amplían el acceso a la Justicia, *Clarín*, 12 October 2009.

Durham, C. (1998) Thoughtful and wordly women: women judges and the law, in: S. Shetreet (Ed) *Women in law* (London/The Hague/Boston, Hebrew University of Jerusalem, Kluwer Law International), pp. 217–236.

Garro, A. (2004) Perspectivas de la Reforma Judicial en América Latina, Democracia, derechos humanos, derechos económicos y sociales, reforma judicial, *El acceso a la justicia como garantía de la igualdad* (BiBlos, Buenos Aires).

Schultz, U. (2013) Do German judges need gender education? in: U. Schultz & G. Shaw (Eds) *Gender and judging* (Oxford, Hart), pp. 585–599.

Raising gender awareness of judges – elements for judicial education in Germany

ULRIKE SCHULTZ
Akad. Oberrätin a.D., FernUniversität in Hagen - Rechtswissenschaftliche Fakultät, Hagen, Germany

ABSTRACT *In Germany no need for gender education in the judiciary is felt. Judges perceive themselves as objective and neutral. Any attempt to deal with gender questions in judicial education tends to be met with hostility. Gender education is however necessary. The question is whether to offer special training or to integrate gender into any kind of judicial education. Careful approaches are necessary. In the following an overview of the situation in Germany is given, and examples of elements used in judicial education are presented.*

Germany has very comprehensive equal opportunities legislation, and gender mainstreaming is a recognized and legally binding principle for the public sector. There are equal opportunities officers and women's advancement plans and gender concepts throughout public institutions as well as the administrative part of the judiciary and the prosecution offices. Gender education, however, is met with distrust, having the odium of ideological re-education, and particularly in the judiciary there is little gender awareness and an aversion against gender training (Schultz, 2013b, p. 595).

Germany is a civil law country with a career judiciary which, through the long and intensive moulding processes in legal education and the selection and promotion procedure, has come to represent a very homogeneous middle class group. Unlike common law judges, civil law judges do not understand their role as a mouthpiece or interpreter of the law, although the application of statutory regulations is less literal than in common law countries with their interpretation acts (Schultz & Shaw, 2013, p. 6). Space for interpretation remains when it comes to applying highly general terms and phrases to specific instances, and mainly in public law (administrative law, social law, tax law) decisions of the authorities are often based on discretion which the judges have to check and evaluate.

Judges enjoy judicial independence, but their personality is hidden behind the institution. Judgments are passed 'in the name of the people' as judgments of court x, y or z. In their view, any thought or talk of subjective elements in their judgments casts doubt on the quality of their legal education and the system as such which they represent (Schultz, 2015).

Gender stereotypes and gendered life experiences can easily have a bearing on the outcome of a case (Schultz, 2003a, 2003b; Schultz & Shaw, 2013), but it is not easy to find overt gender bias, except in postwar cases when conservative 'old men' in the judiciary continued to live and apply outdated models of family life and gender roles (Schultz, 2003c, p. 259 f.). In family law, the notion of gender roles is important, for example in the context of decisions on alimony and custody. In criminal law, the personality of the accused has to be evaluated in the verdict. In labour law, models of male and female competencies may define the working capacities. Even in administrative, social and tax law gender issues play a role. In Germany, in an interplay of family law, labour, tax and social law, the traditional breadwinner model has been cemented, both in the making and in the application of law, an issue which is much discussed, but for which no easy solution is at hand (Schultz, 2013b, p. 590).

Meanwhile close to 50% of judges and prosecutors are women.[1] The question is whether they judge differently from men. There is some evidence that in family law and criminal law gendered sympathies or dislikes on the part of both women and men may influence the results of a case. In made-up files with test cases given to judges in a course on judicial decision-making in the German National Academy for the Judiciary[2] we consistently observed that women tended to pass milder sentences than men. These gender effects, however, are neither reliable nor predictable (Schultz & Shaw, 2013, p. 43).

German judges don't learn about gender issues, neither at university nor during their practical training. Gender and law is not part of the curriculum, and whether gender is mentioned at all depends on the individual law professor[3] (Schultz, 2011). Special lectures on gender and law generally attract only few participants, as law students try to focus on what is necessary to pass their examination. Nor do they want to be stigmatized as attending such 'sectarian' courses. German law students are mainly taught legal doctrine with details of judicature in the core subjects – civil law, criminal law and administrative/constitutional law. However, they do have to deal with equal rights and antidiscrimination issues in the context of constitutional law and European law. The German Federal Constitutional Court has passed many important judgments on equal rights of men and women, many of these due to the initiative of members of the German Women Lawyers Association. In recent years, the focus has been mainly on same-sex, transgender and intersex issues.[4]

I myself have written a gender curriculum for law (2006/2011)[5] in which I have defined educational objectives and identified which issues should be taught in which subjects or fields. I have also proposed adding an introductory course to give students an overarching picture of the relevant questions and structures. The response has been no more than meagre, i.e. one member of a law faculty got back to me with comments.

There is no organized in-service gender training for the judiciary, although the range on offer is vast. The National Academy for the Judiciary offers training places and courses for over 3,000 judges and prosecutors annually,[6] and some federal states have academies of their own[7] or organize further training sessions. Courses mainly deal with practice-related problems and recent legal developments, and so-called behaviour-orientated courses with a focus on communication, including self-reflection. Attendance is voluntary. In recent years, courses on the following subjects with gender implications have been offered: new developments in divorce law for family lawyers (numerous courses), violence in families, how to deal with victims of sexual violence at courts and international trafficking. However, the emphasis tends to be on legal rather than on gender questions. Young judges have to attend a series of accompanying introductory courses on practice skills. None of them comprise elements relating to gender. Guidelines for instructors of courses in leadership for the judiciary in Northrhine-Westfalia do contain a clause requiring the inclusion of gender issues, but it remains unclear whether and in what form this is acted upon (Schultz, 2013b, p. 594 f.).

A couple of years ago a psychologist and I organized two gender training courses at the National Academy, apparently a unique occurrence, and discontinued due to lack of interest. By contrast, courses on career aspects based on the results of our empirical research on Women in Leading Positions in the Judiciary (Schultz *et al.*, 2011; Schultz, 2012, 2013a) were very well received and attended. I built in elements of gender training, namely on gendered communication at court and on subjectivity and gender bias in judging – although this part was always the most difficult to teach. There have also been a couple of courses on 'Women in the Judiciary', dealing more with their life and work situation.

Whenever I am involved in further training for lawyers and judges I refer to gender questions where appropriate. This 'gender inclusive' approach is proving successful. What matters is the methodology. In my experience, judges in further education like entertainment, experiments and playing games, and factual information needs to be interspersed with such activating elements.

In the following I will give an overview of training elements we have used.

Introduction

(1) Do judges have gender stereotypes? No! No?

An example: I had written an editorial for our *Journal for Judges and Prosecutors* in Northrhine-Westfalia based on my research on women in judicial leadership positions (Schultz, 2013a). The (male) judge in charge of editing the piece commented in an email to a female colleague, "Herewith suggestions for the editorial whose style strikes me as masculine and harsh rather than feminine and gentle. Never mind".[8]

Information and discussion

(2) The historical development of women's rights in Germany: from gender wardship to equal status.
(3) Equal rights, equal status, equal standing and antidiscrimination: reflections on sameness and differences.
(4) Leading judgments by the Federal Constitutional Court on equal rights for men and women.
(5) The influence of EU law (the treaties, directives and decisions of the EU Luxembourg Court of Justice) on German equality and antidiscrimination law.
(6) Gender issues in the European Convention on Human Rights, decisions of the European Court of Human Rights, the UN Convention on the Elimination of Discrimination against Women (CEDAW) and other international conventions.
(7) Gender issues in the current legal and political debate (e.g. cuts in alimony, child care, rights in same-sex marriages and partnerships, legal positions of transsexual and intersexual persons, wearing of headscarf or burka in public, obligation for Muslim school girls to take part in gym lessons and swimming instructions, tax benefits for married couples, cuts in social benefits for non-married couples, interpretation of stalking, domestic and sexual violence and rape, asylum or refugee status for women threatened by female genital mutilation, equal pay, quota regulations, parental leave and financial compensation, part-time work in the armed forces).
(8) Gender issues in family law (criminal, labour, administrative, social, tax law).
(9) A statistical picture of the social situation of women and men.
(10) Gender issues in the current gender political debate.
(11) Discretion and sweeping clauses (e.g. fair and just thinking – sec. 242 German Civil Code; good faith, customary practice – sec. 157 German Civil Code) and gender issues.
(12) The professional situation of women in the judiciary, working conditions, career perspectives and gender bias in assessments.

Analysis

(13) Which gender issues have mattered in this . . . judgment? Report and discuss! (Prepare in groups of three or four)

(14) Which gender implications do you find in this act/legal rule? Report and discuss!
(Prepare one rule each or in groups of two) (See addendum)

Exercise

(15) Have you come across gender problems/notions/bias in communication in a typical professional situation?
Try to argue with a colleague.
(Partner exercise with the possibility of video-recording and feedback)
(Reference to Tannen, 1990)

(16) The Alligator River Story: an exercise designed to investigate value-based conflict, decision-making, the challenges of establishing right and wrong with gender perspectives (several versions of the story to be found on the internet, with methodological hints; we use a fairy tale version with a prince and a princess and a sentinel at a bridge).

Activate

(17) Which gender issues do you detect in these ... *pictures*?
(Show pictures, partner work and group discussion)

(18) Gender *implicit association test*, e.g. https://implicit.harvard.edu/implicit/index.jsp
(Individual work, discussion)

(19) Note down on cards gender stereotypes you have come across/people in the street have.
(The cards are being stuck on a painted male or female person on a board at the front)
Discussion. (Carefully: what about your own gender stereotypes?)

(20) Gender quiz
Multiple choice questions of the type:
When did women in Germany get the right to vote? (a) in 1871 with the foundation of the German empire; (b) in 1900, with the passing of the German Civil Code; (c) in 1919, with the Constitution of the Weimar Republic; (d) in 1949, with the Bonn Basic Law? (To be followed up by: when was the first judge admitted? How long were men able to terminate their wives' employment contract? etc. etc.)[9]

Addendum: The new school act

Instruction: Gender check of an act

Does a rule have the **same consequences** for women and men (all)? Check:

- legally
- statistically
- financially
- in case of difference: is there a valid/acceptable reason for it (according to equality rules)?

Do rules take into account

- different **interests** of the sexes/genders?
  e.g. re-evaluation of typical 'female' work
- different **needs** of the sexes/genders?
  e.g. protection against sexual offences/violence

Check **indirect discrimination.**

- direct–indirect discrimination
- indirect: even if a rule is gender neutral, does it affect/disadvantage a majority of one sex/gender?

Are there rules to **balance inequalities?**

- e.g. Employment Advancement Acts
- quota rules
- other rules for redistributionary justice

Application

Which gender implications do you find in the new school act?

New school law

(2) School starts at 9 o'clock.
(3) The school ministry may decide at the end of each term in which school teachers have to work in the following year.
(4) Those who want to work part-time have to agree in writing that they accept to be assigned to any school in the school district.
(5) Disciplinary measures have to be taken my male teachers.
(6) Female teachers may use the parking space close to the entrance door.
(7) Sports lessons have to be offered separately for girls and boys.
(8) For organizational reasons this does not extend to swimming lessons.
(9) Girls have to keep records of their periods and hand them to the sports teacher.
(10) Girls are offered additional math lessons.
(11) School meals are to be prepared by parents. For each pupil a parent has to take on four of these shifts per month.
(12) School fees are waived for final-year students who go on to military service.
(13) Time tables are decided by headmasters.
(14) Teachers are not allowed to wear religious dress at school.
(15) After parental leave attendance at a reintegration course is obligatory.
(16) All pupils have to use their own computer at school.
(17) In case of illness medical assistance is given by a school nurse.

Solutions

(1) School starts at 9 o'clock.

Gender implication: as for most employed people work starts earlier, this is an impediment for fathers and particularly mothers (as women take over more of the domestic duties than men) for their employment.

In Germany, this regulation was proposed to suit the biorhythm of children. (But then: what about the biorhythm of adults?)

(2) The school ministry may decide at the end of each term in which school teachers have to work in the following year.

Job insecurities and threats of unemployment affect women more than men.

I was inspired to propose this regulation by a practice we used to have in the 1980s in Germany. On returning from maternity leave, female teachers did have a job guarantee, but no guarantee of being re-employed at their previous school. Consequently they often ended up in a less attractive school and, worse still, in a school further away from home – which caused many to drop out altogether.

(3) Those who want to work part-time have to agree in writing to accept any teaching post in the school district.

This was a rule practised until well into the twenty-first century.

Similarly, female judges reported that on returning from maternity leave and asking for part-time employment, they were assigned to unattractive positions, organizational needs given as justification.

(4) Disciplinary measures have to be taken by male teachers.

The enforcement of discipline (severe measures) has traditionally been linked to male behaviour. As this conveys an impression of special status, it may become a career factor disadvantaging women.

(5) Female teachers may use the parking space close to the entrance door.

This is a sensible rule and has been applied in Germany for some time. After all, women are more threatened than men by violence and bodily attacks as well as finding it harder to carry heavy loads over longer distances.

(6) Sports lessons have to be offered separately for girls and boys.

This rule has obvious gender implications.

In former times there were separate schools and classes for boys and girls. In the 1970s and 1980s co-education became an aim of educational policies as it was regarded to help boys' classroom discipline. However, in sports lessons boys tended to dominate girls, and sports and exercises preferred by girls – such as gymnastics and dancing – tended to be neglected. Today, girls and boys in their final two years are offered a choice, in most cases confirming the traditional standard pattern soft exercises chosen by girls and rough ones (football, basketball etc.) by boys.

(7) For organizational reasons this does not extend to swimming lessons.

There may indeed be organizational reasons for this rule, e.g. when the class has to be taken by bus to the swimming hall. But there is another gendered aspect in this regulation:

Girls in puberty develop an intensive feeling of shame and may have problems showing their developing bodies in tight sports dresses or particularly bathing suits for fear of being laughed at by the boys or getting indecent comments.

(8) Girls have to keep records of their periods and hand them to the sports teacher.

This is discriminating against girls by making public their periods – although there may be organizational reasons behind it, e.g. if girls try to avoid taking part in sports lessons.

This rule has long applied in German girls' schools. Girls who wanted to be exempted from exercises during their periods had to keep such records and would then sit on a bench watching the others.

(9) Girls are offered additional math lessons.

If only girls are offered additional math training it is taken for granted that they are weaker in math than boys. Additional coaching should be offered to all who need it – boys and girls.

(10) Parents are required to take on the task of cooking school meals – one parent for each pupil doing four shifts a month.

This rule creates problems not only for all parents with day-time jobs, but may also place a heavier burden on mothers (who tend to do the bulk of cooking at home). Additionally, German parents are expected to help with the running of school libraries and cafeterias, tasks which are also mostly performed by women.

(11) School fees are waived for final-year students who go on to military service.

As it applies to both sexes, this rule sounds gender neutral. Yet it may imply hidden or indirect discrimination, as in many countries women are still exempted from doing military service. And if a gender neutral rule affects many more women than men (approx. 80% plus), it represents a case of indirect discrimination.

On the other hand, men embarking on military service are disadvantaged in that their professional training gets delayed or interrupted, although this might be taken to balance out women's classical disadvantage due to a career break for family reasons.

In Germany it was accepted practice – and checked by the administrative and constitutional courts – that young men who had taken their military service got preference in being admitted to study subjects with a numerus clausus, i.e. admission restrictions. In 2011 the military draft was suspended in Germany.

(12) The school director decides on the time table.

At first glance this rule appears gender neutral. But if the school director is a man, he may be unaware of time problems experienced by women and particularly mothers. Therefore it would make more sense to set up a small timetabling committee composed of an equal number of men and women.

(13) Teachers are not allowed to wear religious dress at school.

Although this rule is phrased in a gender neutral manner – it could extend to monks/priests as well as nuns – it has a clear gender implication, as it includes women who want to wear the Muslim headscarf. In, for example, France there is a clear segregation between religion/church and state and therefore any kind of religious dress in state schools is prohibited – also for pupils. In Germany the administrative and constitutional courts in most federal states have decided that the headscarf infringes the (political and religious) neutrality required of teachers, thus potentially excluding Muslim women from practising the profession, at least in state schools. However, the wearing of headscarves is permitted for pupils.

(14) After parental leave a reintegration course is obligatory.

On the one hand, such a course may be helpful. But on the other hand, it may disadvantage the career prospects of those affected (currently still mainly women).

(15) Pupils have to use their own computer at school.

This rule may again have a hidden discrimination if more boys than girls own a computer.

(16) In case of illness medical assistance is given by a school nurse.

Have you immediately thought of a woman? As most nurses are women? Please question your own stereotypical perceptions. A school nurse could also be a man. The question in this regulation is whether it is a problem for boys to be treated by a woman or the other way round for girls to be treated by a man. Here we have an accepted practice that people can be treated by a medical person from the other sex.

But maybe you see this differently.

I was inspired to construct these examples by cases I know from Germany and other European countries. You may find in the cases more hidden gender implications.

- Can you find other rules with gender implications?

Disclosure statement

No potential conflict of interest was reported by the author.

Notes

[1] The Federal statistics show for women judges a 40% share of the total workload, for prosecutors 41% (1 January 2013). As many women work part-time, the number of women calculated by 'heads' is

higher. On 1 January 2014, Northrhine-Westfalia had just under 46% female judges and 48% female prosecutors. Their numbers still keep on rising.

[2] Our sample contained approximately 250 participants of whom about 35% were women. The cases tested the so-called ‘anchor effect’ in decision-making. If a high or low sum or punishment is mentioned at the start of dealing with a case, the result will be oriented to this amount or figure, which means that an initial statement of a mild punishment will lead to a milder sentence than an initial mention of a harsh punishment; cf. Englich and Mussweiler (2001).

[3] The interviews for our women law professors project (www.fernuni-hagen.de/jurpro) showed that among the women law professors (who make up less than 15% of the total number) some gender awareness can be expected, which does not necessarily mean that it translates into their academic writing or teaching.

[4] There are also important judgments by the European Court of Justice in Luxembourg on the legal situation in Germany in these matters and by the European Court of Human Rights in Strasbourg.

[5] See http://www.gender-curricula.com/gender-curricula/. An English version can be obtained from me.

[6] There are an estimated 5,560 prosecutors and an estimated 21,600 judges for an 80 million population (1 January 2013) for an 80 million population. The programme is accessible via the internet at http://www.deutsche-richterakademie.de

[7] By far the largest of these academies is that of Northrhine-Westfalia, the biggest federal state with 18 million inhabitants and 4,913 judges (1 January 2014). Its programme can also be found on the internet at http://www.jak.nrw.de/

[8] Her comment: “Take it easy, take dynamite!” Alternative: “What about: Men Don’t Listen and Women Can’t Read Maps?” [title of a bestseller by Allan Pease and Barbara Pease (2001)].

[9] Methodological hint: with large groups you can label the four corners of the room A, B, C and D and tell participants to move each time to the corner with the letter of their chosen alternative. Even senior judges liked it. Don’t forget a prize!

References

Englich, B. & Mussweiler, T. (2001) Sentencing under uncertainty: anchoring effects in the courtroom, *Journal of Applied Social Psychology*, 31, pp. 1535–1551.

Pease, A. & Pease, B. (2001) *Why Men don’t Listen & Women can’t Read Maps* (London: Orion).

Schultz, U. (2003a) Women in the world’s legal professions: overview and synthesis, in: U. Schultz & G. Shaw (Eds) *Women in the World’s Legal Professions* (Oxford, Hart), pp. xxv–lxii.

Schultz, U. (2003b) Women lawyers in Germany: perception and construction of femininity, in: U. Schultz & G. Shaw (Eds) *Women in the World’s Legal Professions* (Oxford: Hart), pp. 295–321.

Schultz, U. (2003c) Geschlechterbilder der älteren Herren des Bundesgerichtshofs, in: Reader für die Aktionswochen der kommunalen Gleichstellungsbeauftragten 2003 (Ed) *Frauen und Recht* (Düsseldorf, The Ministry of Health, Social Matters, Women and Family NRW), pp. 259–260.

Schultz, U. (2011) Legal Education in Germany - an ever (never?) ending story of resistance to change. In *RED, Revista de Educación y Dere*cho, n. 4. http://revistes.ub.edu/index.php/RED

Schultz, U. (2012) Frauen in Führungspositionen der Justiz. Eine Untersuchung von Frauenkarrieren in den Justizbehörden in Nordrhein-Westfalen, *Deutsche Richterzeitung (DRiZ)*, 90, pp. 264–272.

Schultz, U. (2013a) “I was noticed and I was asked ... ” Women’s careers in the Judiciary. Results of an empirical study for the ministry of justice in Northrhine-Westfalia, Germany, in: U. Schultz and G. Shaw (Eds) *Gender and Judging* (Oxford: Hart), pp. 145–166.

Schultz, U. (2013b) Do German judges need gender education? in: U. Schultz & G. Shaw (Eds) *Gender and Judging* (Oxford: Hart), pp. 585–598.

Schultz, U. (2015) Do female judges judge differently? in: M. Lindbekk & N. Sonneveld (Eds) *Women Judges in the Muslim World* (Leiden, Brill), forthcoming.

Schultz, U. & Shaw, G. (2013) Introduction: gender and judging: overview and synthesis, in: U. Schultz & G. Shaw (Eds) *Gender and Judging* (Oxford: Hart), pp. 3–47.

Schultz, U., Peppmeier, I. & Rudek, A. (2011) *Frauen in Führungspositionen der Justiz. Eine Untersuchung der Bedingungen von Frauenkarrieren in den Justizbehörden in Nordrhein-Westfalen* (Projektbericht, Hagen, Institut für Geschlechterforschung und Gleichstellungsrecht und –politik).
Tannen, D. (1990) *You Just Don't Understand: Women and Men in Conversation* (New York: Ballantine).

Judicial education on 'gender awareness' in Australia

JOHN BASTEN
New South Wales Court of Appeal, Sydney, Australia

ABSTRACT *In Australia, as elsewhere, cultural blindness to difference based on gender can affect the impartiality of judging. It is an important aspect of the unstated assumptions on which judges act and which they need to examine. This is especially so where the assumptions are a reflection of dominant social attitudes and values. Judges are expected to apply community values, so long as they are consistent with equality before the law. Blatant examples of gender bias tend to diminish as diversity increases, both within the judiciary and within the legal profession. Stereotyping assumptions can be explored through judicial education, but Australian experience suggests that programmes will only receive a receptive audience if sensitive to concerns about judicial independence. To that end, discussion may best be located within the boundaries of the broader topic of unconscious partiality. Steps being taken in New South Wales to raise gender sensitivity are noted.*

Introduction

As demonstrated by the book of papers published recently by Ulrike Schultz and Gisela Shaw (Schultz & Shaw, 2013, p. 3), there is a wealth of research being conducted on gender awareness in the judiciary in many countries in Asia, South America, Africa, Europe, North America and Australasia. The work undertaken in Japan by Kayo Minamino and her colleagues exemplifies the breadth of that research (Minamino, 2013, p. 543).

An important preliminary lesson from this research is that, broadly speaking, lack of gender awareness is a problem across different cultures and across different legal systems, but is revealed in different forms; it follows that solutions which will work in one country may fail or be inappropriate in another. That is exactly as one should expect. The lesson applies to me too; I can describe my perceptions of our

Anglo/Australian experience, but I cannot (and should not) extrapolate to other legal cultures.

There is a fundamental reason why all countries which operate under the political principle of the rule of law share the problem. The reason is that laws must be applied, in the words of our judicial oath, without fear or favour, affection or ill will. Partiality, that is preferring one party over another for reasons not permitted by law, is prohibited. Judges must be impartial at all times and in all cases: at least, that is the ideal. Sometimes we fall short; and in particular we may fall short because we carry unexamined 'baggage'.[1] Part of the baggage, and I emphasise *part*, especially for male judges, is an omission, a lack of appreciation of the experiences of, and values which are commonly held by, women. There are other points of blindness, but this one is particularly important because it potentially affects half the population.

There are a number of assumptions underlying the concept of judicial education with respect to gender awareness. Any proposal directed to this topic must first identify and address those assumptions. One assumption is that differences in gender can affect the way judges administer justice and decide cases. No doubt that is true, but how it works, and why this issue deserves special attention, require consideration.

Having said that culture and the legal system are significant variables in understanding and addressing this issue, let me say a little about our Australian context.

The Australian context

Australian courts (like those in the English tradition elsewhere) are largely constituted by judicial officers who are not trained as such, but are lawyers with many years' experience in practice, whether private, public or self-employed. Whilst, in the past, magistrates were part of the public service and obtained experience as clerks of the relevant courts, that is no longer the case. Like judges in higher courts, they are chosen from the ranks of practising lawyers, operate independently of government and are appointed to a statutory retirement age (usually 70).[2]

Once appointed, a judge can be removed only by the parliament, and not by the executive government alone, and then only for misbehaviour or incapacity.[3] Generally, judges are not promoted and expect no preferment. Once appointed, most will remain in that position until retirement. They will acquire seniority and respect based on performance, but they expect that from peers and not from the government.

Our laws may best be described as a mixture of judge-made law and statutes enacted by parliament. There is room for interpretation and for discretionary judgment in their application. Trial judges (as everywhere) must apply their skills and experience in assessing the evidence, particularly in relation to witnesses giving oral accounts of what they have seen or done, or what has happened to them.

Finally, a special feature of our system of administering justice should be noted. Trials of serious criminal charges are conducted before a judge and jury of 12 drawn from the community. The jury are solely responsible for fact-finding – applying legal principles explained to them by the presiding judge, but assessing the witnesses based on their diverse experiences. Juries contain roughly equal proportions of men and women. The jury has an important constitutional function in the administration of justice. They are not specifically instructed in how to avoid prejudice and stereotyping in relation to gender.

Identifying the issues

Gender supplies an important consideration for judges in four respects. Firstly, there are gender-based values which infuse substantive legal principles. Much academic writing has focused on this aspect (Graycar & Morgan, 2002). It is one of which judicial officers should be conscious, but which they have little opportunity to change. Secondly, there are areas for evaluative judgment where consciousness of gender-based values may be significant. Assessment of damages in tort and sentencing for crimes may provide examples. Thirdly, gender may be relevant to our expectations of how people behave in particular circumstances. In this sense our understanding of typical responses (what people in fact do, rather than how they should be treated) will affect our assessment of credibility. Fourthly, the last issue arises with respect to how juries assess credibility and thus the directions to be given by the judge. The jury should be warned about problems of which they may not be aware (e.g. unreliability of identification evidence) but to warn of inappropriate gender stereotyping may be to intrude on the core function of the jury. It is the second and third aspects which engage the core issue for present purposes.

There is no doubt that in many respects men and women share the same experiences and skills. However, there are areas in which experience and (some would say) skills and methods of reasoning differ. Based on personal experience, culture and upbringing, people acquire different values and assess the world differently. On the other hand, as judges, there is much which is likely to unite us in our common training as lawyers.[4]

The fact that judges bring their own values and experience of the world to the function of judging (possibly in varying degrees) has been the subject of concern over the decades and, indeed, through much of the twentieth century. The early modern expressions were found in the area of industrial law, and not only in complaints from workers (Scrutton, 1921, p. 8). The assumption was that by background and upbringing, judges were more likely to be understanding of the values and goals of employers than those of labourers and unionists. A similar concern arose in relation to race. The civil rights movement in the USA, for example, had its own analysis of the composition and operation of courts.

Recognition of gender as a point of difference appears, broadly, to have arisen later than class and ethnicity, and has been followed by concerns expressed by various social minorities, including gay men and lesbians (Mahoney, 1993, p. 199).

To place gender concerns in a list is not to diminish their validity, but to seek to understand the role which gender awareness may properly play in educational programmes. Much advocacy for oppressed groups relies on an assumption that a judge's membership of a particular group, at least where that group is not part of the dominant class in society, is a condition of full understanding and hence of providing justice. The move for recognition of the special needs of oppressed or excluded groups thus tends to be expressed, not as a demand for judicial education, but for representation.

Diversity – the composition of courts

'Representation' may be appropriate in a legislature, but the executive and the judiciary should *reflect*, rather than represent, the diversity of the society they serve. Diversity is an important value in the administration of justice. Whilst the rule of law may depend on the availability of mechanisms for enforcement (such as an effective and uncorrupted police force, and sheriff's officers to enforce civil judgments) it will also depend upon a high measure of acceptance, across all social groupings, of the functioning of courts. Thus, in a civil society based upon notions of individual equality, the apparent exclusion of a large and highly visible group from the judiciary will tend to diminish respect for the law and undermine the rule of law as a political institution. The presence of women on courts in significant numbers is a necessary element of a healthy democracy.

There is a wealth of anecdotal evidence that women appearing as advocates feel uncomfortable and perceive themselves to be outsiders in courtrooms routinely presided over by male judges. To describe the feeling as a 'perception' is not to imply that it is unjustified. The feelings of exclusion may extend to female judges, at least when few in number, for example, in the atmosphere of the dining room at court (Darbyshire, 2011, p. 423).

In Australia, approximately 33% of judicial officers are women and that percentage applies across almost all jurisdictions (state and federal) and at all levels in the judicial hierarchy, although it tends to be lower in the higher courts (AIJA, 2014; McColl, 2014). (That achievement has occurred entirely within my adult life: when I graduated from university, there was only one female judge in the superior courts in Australia, Dame Roma Mitchell, who was appointed to the Supreme Court of South Australia in 1965.)

However, the importance of maintaining a reasonable proportion of women in the judiciary is not limited to democratic inclusivity. Although not the primary justification for maintaining a diverse judiciary, women may have an educative function for the judiciary as a whole. That effect will operate differently in different jurisdictions. Thus, our court of appeal, excluding the Chief Justice whose sitting time is limited, and excluding the chief judges of the trial divisions who also rarely sit on appeals, has a President (who is a woman) and nine other fulltime judges of appeal, of whom two are female. We sit in benches of three, so that the chance of a male judge sitting with a female colleague is high. To the extent that a woman's view of a matter were to be significantly different from that of her male colleagues, she is able to express that view, not merely in a judgment, but in discussions that occur both in court and out of court. Of course, that involvement is not available in trial courts, where judges sit alone. The two trial divisions of our Supreme Court comprise approximately 36 fulltime judges, of whom six are women. One division hears serious crime and civil negligence cases, while the other deals with much of the commercial work of the court (and has a female chief judge). Although the numbers are perhaps lower than one might wish, there is still a group of female judges whose views will be expressed to their colleagues from time to time, including in the course of informal discussions about their respective cases and during regular lunches.

I derive two propositions from the experience of our court. The first is that the need for judicial education regarding gender awareness is likely to be reduced in circumstances where women constitute a significant proportion of a court. Secondly, and perhaps ironically, judicial education with respect to gender awareness is likely to be taken more seriously, and thus likely to be more effective, where there is a significant number of women on the court. However, there appears to be a 'critical mass', below which women judges are likely to feel themselves to be outsiders and uncomfortable (Darbyshire, 2011, p. 423). (That is not to say that achievement of such an outcome is a sufficient response to the need for diversity; nor that it is possible to define that level – either in numerical terms, or across courts.)

The importance of a gender-neutral court

The literature assumes that gender awareness, as an element in judicial education, is intended to address the needs of male judges for insights as to female values and experiences. As a broad proposition, and in the present social context, that focus should be accepted. The introduction of sex discrimination laws in Australia was accompanied by a debate as to whether they should apply both to discrimination against women and discrimination against men. The principle of formal equality suggested that they should apply to both; the goal of substantive equality suggested that men do not need protective laws of that kind, because they generally have enjoyed a position of superiority, rather than inferiority, in the public life of the country.

Sexual assault is often identified as a situation where many men and many women could (and undoubtedly do) have different perspectives. But the courtroom brings its own set of values. Assuming a male accused and a female complainant (the most usual case) it would undermine the rule of law if the outcome were thought to depend on whether the judge was male or female. And race can add another dimension (*R v. S (RD)* [1997]). Diversity may, by raising such questions, highlight the complacency of assumed impartiality in another age. The only appropriate response is to ensure that it does *not* matter who the judge is. The principle of impartiality does not assume a mind free of personal opinions and values, but rather an ability to recognise, question and consciously allow for the attitudes and sympathies which are held, when deciding a particular case.[5] To that end, judges must be able to discuss, identify and explore assumptions, attitudes and values. To provide a forum for that to happen is an important function of judicial education.

The way in which judges behave in court can be critical to the perception of equal treatment according to law. Any person involved in court proceedings who is treated dismissively is likely to believe they have not been accorded 'a fair go'. Comments by male judges revealing misogynist or stereotyping views have no place in any courtroom. Although it is not part of this topic, there should be scope for complaints to an independent panel which can review judicial conduct.[6]

One would like to think that such concerns are relics of bygone days, but they clearly are not, or at least not everywhere. On the other hand, most male judges on our court have grown up in an era when it was not unusual to appear with or against female advocates, to be briefed by female solicitors and to appear (at least on occasion) before female judges. Further, many of us live with professionals. In the last decade the number of partners of judges on our court who have held (and often continue to hold) positions in business, government or as self-employed professionals, has increased dramatically.

Expectations and understanding will be affected by such changes in demography. Several factors work together; however, the most important factor in terms of avoiding social ostracism is probably the sheer weight of numbers. Once women exceed a figure around 20%–25% of the court's membership, appearing before a female judge is likely to be seen as 'normal'. Through various processes, the atmosphere in the courtroom is likely to change from the earlier days when a male ethos dominated.

Attitudes can be held subliminally and may be retained despite such changes. These may require conscious exposure, but when exposed may readily be addressed.

Gender and decision-making

The processes of decision-making and judgment writing may be distinguished from issues relating to conduct in court and the atmosphere of the courtroom. Whether women judges decide cases and write judgments differently from men is controversial,[7] as is the proposition that there should be education to teach men these skills, implying that they are a preferred form of judging. Of course, if gender is (or should be) reflected in decision-making, it must be discussed in judicial education.

In the English-speaking world, the issue was clearly articulated in a paper by Justice Bertha Wilson, the first woman appointed to the Supreme Court of Canada (in 1982). Prior to attaining that high office, she had been a judge on the Ontario Court of Appeal since 1975. In 1990, with some 15 years' experience on superior courts, she wrote a paper entitled 'Will Women Judges Really Make a Difference?' (Wilson, 1990).

Over the 24 years since Justice Wilson published this paper, the intensity of interest in the question she identified has grown exponentially, at least if measured by academic research and publications (Schultz & Shaw, 2013). The answers to this question may be important in determining the scope and content of judicial education in the current era.

At one level, the question may readily be answered, yes. A critical mass of women judges will make a difference in the ways already identified. By reflecting one of the most obvious elements of diversity in every society, their presence will help to overcome the sense of disenfranchisement which inevitably results from the absence of women from any of the three arms of government. By the same token, their presence will lend credibility to the administration of justice. There will be consequential effects, including the reduction (and hopefully the removal) of feelings of alienation felt by women working within the legal profession and the courts. The importance of these consequences should not be underestimated; they are likely to build on themselves.

There is another sense in which the inclusion of women in the judiciary may well affect the outcomes in some cases. For the reasons already explained, all of us bring certain values to the administration of justice, which will be based to a significant extent on our life experiences. Arguably, maturity and a range of life experience should be criteria for judicial selection. Further, the desirability of a range of experience across the membership of a court is also a relevant consideration. (Some differences in experience may diminish as women become familiar in the corridors of power, whether political, governmental or commercial. Biological roles will not change, but aspects of oppression may diminish.)

Justice Wilson's question, however, was primarily directed at a different level. It was intended to focus on whether cases will be decided differently when the judiciary contains a significant female membership. At that level, the question itself is fraught, for a number of reasons. First, it must not be allowed to influence the identified need for diversity in the composition of the courts. By analogy, democratic government requires that women have the vote. Although psephologists treat gender as an important factor in studying voting patterns, women should have the vote whether that would affect the outcome of elections or have no influence at all on the outcome of any election or all elections. By parity of reasoning, a conclusion that women judges will not affect the way in which cases are decided does not mean that increasing the numbers of women in the judiciary is not an important goal, or even that it is a goal having a lower priority than it otherwise might.

The question is reflected in feminist literature which seeks to locate specifically feminist sets of values which, to form a social goal, must be both different from and superior to the values presently in place. Justice Wilson (1990, pp. 519–520) drew on the work of Professor Gilligan (1982) in search of such values. Justice Wilson (1990, p. 520) noted:

> Gilligan's work on conceptions of morality among adults suggests that women's ethical sense is significantly different from men's. Men see moral problems as arising from competing rights; the adversarial process comes easily to them. Women see moral problems as arising from competing obligations, the one to the other; the important thing is to preserve relationships, to develop an ethic of caring. The goal, according to women's ethical sense, is not seen in terms of winning or losing but, rather, in terms of achieving an optimum outcome for all individuals involved in the moral dilemma. It is not difficult to see how this contrast in thinking might form the basis of different perceptions of justice.

Other work has focused on women's superior skills in listening, empathising and communicating (Cain, 1988, p. 1954; Wilson, 1990, p. 521).

There are risks of unintended consequences attending this line of argument. Supposing empirical research provided support for the psychological theory, the response would surely be to ask where people with these specialist capabilities are best deployed. The answer is likely to be the trial courts and particularly the magistrates' courts and tribunals with the greatest contact with members of the public. Indeed, there might be a tendency to have women focus on alternative dispute resolution, thus creating a new pressure for women to work outside the mainstream courts. Once established, such a mindset would operate adversely to the interests of the many women in the profession who specialise in constitutional law, commercial law, intellectual property, taxation and land law.[8]

Further, the argument that experience affects outcomes justifies inquiry into the judge's experiences, with the purpose of seeking recusal for apprehended bias if the information gleaned warrants such an application. Public confidence in the judiciary is likely to be diminished, rather than enhanced, by such inquiries and applications. Our system depends on judges identifying potential conflicts and either not sitting, or advising the parties of the issue and seeing if objection is taken. However, recusal is usual only in cases of specific connection, such as knowing a witness or a party or involvement in related litigation when credibility of a person was assessed, or having acted for a party before appointment to the bench.

Otherwise, judges are expected to put personal views on matters other than relevant legal principles to one side, so as to reach a decision on the evidence and according to law. Judicial education is devoted to the realisation of the ideal that the identity of the judge should not affect the outcome. As between the parties, he or she should strive for neutrality, although the outcome will not be neutral.

If the established legal principles do not fairly reflect values of gender equality, the proper way to promote those values is to identify them and seek to adapt the system by legislation. Indeed that has happened in one of the areas identified by Justice Wilson, namely the "complex system of exclusionary evidential rules" which she equated with an adversarial system reflecting male values. Whether or not that characterisation is correct, there have been major reforms of the rules of evidence since 1990 (at least in Australia) which appear to have had nothing to do with the appointment of more women to the bench, as opposed to broader political pressure on legislatures. Some of the exclusionary rules are designed to protect criminal defendants from juries convicting on the basis of prejudice and stereotyping, rather than by focusing (as they should) strictly on evidence directed to the charge laid by the prosecution. There have been changes in recent years in Australia with respect to aspects of criminal procedure designed to reduce the need for complainants in sexual assault cases to relive the experience in a very public forum and before an alleged attacker. They have not been uniformly welcomed, but they have resulted from a public debate and legislative response.

This brief review of concerns raised about the role of women in the judiciary (or more accurately their absence) reveals two matters of importance for judicial education, one involving removal of a negative element, the other a positive benefit. First, while attitudes are changing, there are still too many examples in our country of male judges with unconscious stereotypical attitudes about the role of women in society. Those attitudes, it may be noted, do not necessarily relate to the role of women as judges or lawyers, or as professionals more generally. Thus, a judge who is genuinely and consistently respectful of the views of female colleagues may yet make inappropriate assumptions about women involved in sexual assault cases or women seeking a greater share of a testator's estate. It is desirable for all of us to examine our unconscious thought patterns. By providing structured assistance in this regard, judicial education may be seen as an attempt to counter negative influences.

The second matter is that women's different life experiences and consequential values, if incorporated into judicial decision-making, may complement a judge's frame of reference. Education directed to that end may be seen as promoting a positive benefit, as well as removing a taint on impartiality. (The distinction is no doubt one of emphasis rather than a comparison of absolutes; nevertheless, it may be important in how programmes for judges are presented.)

Judicial education in Australia

This discussion appears to raise a paradox: addressing partiality in the form of unconscious prejudices requires some form of judicial education – a process which has the capacity to intrude on judicial independence. This apparent paradox can be resolved. To explain how, it is necessary to look at some history and context.

For a long period, there was resistance to 'judicial education' as a legitimate activity. That attitude was based on a concern that any kind of 'education' diminished the independence of the judiciary. That was an unsophisticated view from a simpler age. It is now necessary to acknowledge the growing complexity of law and society, which calls for continuing professional education.

Nevertheless, there are limits as to what is acceptable. Discussing how kinds of cases should be addressed is acceptable; direction as to how particular cases should be decided is not. Identifying the skill sets required for judging is acceptable; criticism of individual judges (except of course through appellate judgments) is likely to raise resistance. Anything which carries the hint of political direction will be greeted with deep suspicion.

Yet feminism is a set of political values. Most judges will understand it to be a reflection of the principle of equality and thus in conformity with the rule of law. But as an ideology it has no direct application in legal reasoning, nor is it a requirement for judicial education.[9] A pragmatic approach to gender awareness is to locate it firmly in the broader concept of unconscious partiality. It is then an acceptable (and essential) element of judicial education.

It is somewhat artificial to look for a defining commencement date for moves to introduce gender awareness into judicial education in Australia. That is for two reasons. The first is that whatever date one chooses was preceded by laws relating to sex discrimination generally and many other public activities devoted to promoting equality for women.

The literature suggests that the topic of gender awareness was stimulated in Australia by the writings and speeches of various Canadian lawyers, including Professor Kathleen Mahoney, a distinguished Canadian academic.

In 1990 Chief Justice David Malcolm, from Western Australia, attended an international conference in Edinburgh entitled 'Equality and the Administration of Justice: Gender, Race and Class' (Malcolm, 1993, p. 194). [A similar positive response to that conference was noted by Justice North of the Federal Court (*Sun v. Minister for Immigration and Ethnic Affairs* 1997).] Stimulated by the presentations at that conference, including from Professor Mahoney, he organised a seminar on the topic 'Gender Bias in the Administration of Justice' held at the Supreme Court of Western Australia on 14 August 1992. He also established a committee to consider the question of gender bias, which reported in 1994 (*Chief Justice's Taskforce*, 1994, Ch. 3).

In the same period, the Senate in the Commonwealth Parliament asked the Standing Committee on Legal and Constitutional Affairs to inquire into 'gender bias' and the judiciary, which resulted in a report dated May 1994 (Australian Parliament, 1994).

Much has changed over the last 20 years. Now, three specific propositions should be borne in mind. One is that judges value high quality judicial education but tend to be impatient with, and dismissive of, that which does not live up to their expectations. That proposition flows from two somewhat conflicting factors. On the one hand, when appointed, our judges tend to be highly experienced lawyers, senior in their profession, both in terms of professional status and age. On the other hand, most of us will readily acknowledge that the function of a judge is not something that we have experience of, and will concede the need for assistance.

A second and related point is that many judges will come from a specialist background of legal practice, as to which they are truly expert, but will be required as judges to function across a far broader range of cases. The need to become familiar with new areas of law and procedure and write authoritative judgments about them is a demanding exercise.

The third point is that many lawyers who become judges will have skills drawn from professional and personal experience. They will probably have spent much time in their professional careers assessing the truthfulness and reliability of witnesses (and clients) and forming judgments about how others will view them as witnesses in court. However, the more senior one is professionally, the more likely one is to resist the suggestion that one has unconscious prejudices, unarticulated and unexamined values, and limited understanding of how one reaches one's own decisions and makes one's own judgments. Yet this is the area into which judicial education must delve if there is to be any serious attempt to improve levels of general awareness.

In New South Wales, the most focused attempts to raise gender sensitivity are to be found in the Bench Book, *Equality Before the Law* produced by the Judicial Commission of New South Wales (2006) with the assistance of a panel of judicial officers. It was not the first of its kind; *Equal Treatment* Bench Books had been published earlier in Queensland and the UK. Ours has been updated from time to time since its initial publication in 2006. It draws upon the precedents in other jurisdictions and papers given at earlier national judicial orientation programmes.

The Bench Book is provided to all judicial officers within New South Wales. It contains sections on numerous groups and issues, including Indigenous people, people from non-English-speaking backgrounds, people with particular religious affiliations, with disabilities, and young people as well as gender issues. The section on women commences with some general statistics about the social status, employment and education of women. It identifies sources of inequality, stating:

> Women tend to fare worse than men in relation to their employment status, income level, the amount of unpaid household work and childcare activities they engage in, the type and nature of violence committed against them, and in relation to some legal proceedings.

Troublingly, the Bench Book notes:

> It is also the experience of the Judicial Commission of NSW and other complaint bodies that many more women than men complain of gender bias in relation to the legal system and legal proceedings.
>
> It is true that not all women fare badly in comparison to men, or feel discriminated against in comparison with men. However, the general existence of gender inequality or bias in our society means that, for many women, unless appropriate account is taken of the examples of gender bias listed ... below, a woman may:
>
> - feel uncomfortable, resentful or offended by what occurs in court;
> - feel that an injustice has occurred
> - in some cases be treated unfairly and/or unjustly.

The Bench Book then lists and addresses a number of situations where gender bias could occur, or be perceived to occur:

> (1) using language and terminology carelessly and/or inappropriately – that is, using language, statements or comments that create, or could create, a perception of gender bias;
> (2) assessing a woman against how a man would have acted or felt in that situation;
> (3) assessing a woman against how a 'normal' woman ought to behave;
> (4) showing a lack of understanding of the nature of domestic violence or sexual assault, and/or of the impact of domestic violence or sexual assault on women;
> (5) showing a lack of understanding of the value of household work and childcare activities;
> (6) not taking appropriate account of the statistical differences between men and women in relation to such matters as income level, household work and child care activities, and
> (7) implying that a woman makes a less credible witness than a man.

Many of the examples are culturally quite specific; others are almost simplistic. For example, we advise judges not to address women by their given names if they address men using a title and a family name. Some topics deal with modes of address in court; others with assumptions which may underlie the assessment of evidence, such as the extent to which it is practicable for a woman to leave a violent partner. Further, in major criminal trials a judge presides, but fact-finding is undertaken by a 12-person jury. Other matters dealt with in the Bench Book concern directions to be given to jurors in considering the evidence. While the use of lay jurors in criminal trials is derived from long-established British tradition and provides many in the community with a direct role in administering criminal justice, jurors will bring to their task both everyday experience and everyday prejudices. Possible prejudices may need to be addressed by directions from the judge.

Beyond the circulation to all judicial officers of the *Equality* Bench Book, the topic of gender awareness is dealt with incidentally in seminars organised by the Judicial Commission for the courts and at annual court conferences. In our court, we are focusing on understanding the psychology of decision-making and how unconscious biases can (and in some circumstances undoubtedly will) affect the way we make decisions and thus administer justice.

Conclusions

Most judges have a limited role in leading social change; our primary function is to administer the law, rather than make it. However, administering the law frequently involves evaluation and choices, and judicial education can at least help to prevent judges from preserving or reinforcing factors which diminish the equal treatment of women in society. There is an increasing insistence that partiality is more than conscious bias. A truly impartial judge must be able to identify and counter unconscious prejudices, stereotyping and predilections. However, the line between sound judgment and prejudice is porous and contestable. It is an important function of judicial education to raise awareness of such issues, of which gender difference is an important part.

The dangers of unconscious prejudice for true impartiality were recognised long before the concept of 'judicial education' became acceptable in common-law countries. The appropriate solution was then seen to be self-examination, itself a desirable (if not an essential) skill for a good judge.[10] However, the place of continuing legal education within the legal profession is now well-established (and is a requirement for annual recertification). Thus, our judges, who were practitioners prior to appointment, are amenable to the idea of continuing legal education once appointed to a court.

The important protection against any intrusion on judicial independence is to ensure that control of judicial education lies with the judges themselves. Thus, our court has a committee of judges which organises educational programmes, with the help of a Judicial Commission, which is itself governed by a Board comprising the heads of all jurisdictions.

The Australian Council of Chief Justices has approved a goal that judges participate in 5 days of continuing education a year (National Judicial College of Australia, 2010, p. 29). Attendance is entirely voluntary, but, at least in New South Wales, it is well-attended and appreciated.

The issues in civil-law jurisdictions with a career judiciary are beyond the scope of this paper and beyond my competence to discuss. The principle of impartiality will not be foreign to those jurisdictions, but questions of independence will operate differently.

Acknowledgements

This is a revised version of a paper presented at Kyoto International Conference on Judicial Training for Gender Fairness in the Courts, Kyoto Women's University, Kyoto, Japan, 12–13 April 2014. Valuable research assistance was provided by my clerk, Steven Gardiner.

Disclosure statement

No potential conflict of interest was reported by the author.

Notes

[1] Elias (2012, p. 402); *Liteky v. United States* 114 S. Ct 1147 (1994) at 1155 (Scalia J); *R v S (RD)* [1997] 3 SCR 484 at [35], L'Heureux-Dube and McLachlin JJ quoting the Canadian Judicial Council (1991); and Cardozo (1921, pp. 12–13, 167).

[2] In New South Wales and Tasmania, the retirement age is 72: *Judicial Officers Act 1986* (NSW), ss 44(1) and (3); *Supreme Court Act 1887* (Tas) s 6A(1); *Magistrates Court Act 1987* (Tas) s 9(4)(a). For all others (except magistrates in WA and ACT) it is 70: *The Constitution*, s 72; *Federal Circuit Court of Australia Act 1999* (Cth) ss 9 & Sch 1, Pt 1, cl 1(4); *Supreme Court of Queensland Act 1991* (Qld) s 23(1); *District Court of Queensland Act 1967* (Qld) s 14(1); *Magistrates Act 1991* (Qld) s 42(d); *Supreme Court Act 1935* (SA) s 13A(1); *District Court Act 1991* (SA) s 16(1); *Magistrates Act 1983* (SA) s 9(1)(c); *Constitution Act 1975* (Vic) s 77(3); *County Court Act 1958* (Vic) ss 8(3), 14(1)(b), 14(1)(c); *Magistrates' Court Act 1989* (Vic) s 12(a); *Judges' Retirement Act 1937* (WA) s 3; *District Court of Western Australia Act 1969* (WA) s 16; *Supreme Court Act 1993* (ACT) s 4(3); *Supreme Court Act 1979* (NT) s 38; *Magistrates Act 1979* (NT) s 7(1). For magistrates in WA and ACT the age is 65: *Magistrates Court Act 2004* (WA) s 5 & Sch 1, cl 11(1)(a); *Magistrates Court Act 1930* (ACT) s 7D(1).

[3] *Australian Constitution*, s 72(ii); *Constitution Act 1902* (NSW), s 53; *Constitution of Queensland 2001* (Qld), s 61; *Constitution Act 1975* (Vic), s 87AAB; *Judicial Commissions Act 1994* (ACT), s 5(1); *Supreme Court 1979* (NT) s 40(1). South Australia, Tasmania and Western Australia do not prescribe grounds for removal: *Constitution Act 1934* (SA), s 75; *Supreme Court (Judges' Independence) Act 1857* (Tas), s 1; *Supreme Court Act 1935* (WA), s 9.

[4] Mack and Roach Anleu (2013, Ch. 2.5, p. 211) reporting recent empirical research on how female judicial officers in Australia view their roles.

[5] *R v S (RD)* [1997] 3 S.C.R. 484 at [35] (L'Heureux-Dube and McLachlin JJ) and [119] (Cory J).

[6] In New South Wales, this is one function of the Judicial Commission, which has a complaint handling role (the Conduct Division) quite separate from its role in providing judicial education: see *Judicial Officers Act 1986* (NSW), Parts 5 and 6.

[7] See Rackley (2013) reporting an exercise stimulated by Lord Neuberger, President of the UK Supreme Court, enquiring whether a detectable difference could be found between the judgments authored by women and those authored by men. The answer was largely negative: the exercise appears to have identified more by way of stereotyping assumptions on the part of the readers as to how women judges would write.

[8] These concerns as to unintended consequences echo the analysis of Professor Rosalind Dixon (now at the University of New South Wales) in an assessment of female appointees to the US Supreme Court (Dixon, 2010). See also Cooney (1993, p. 25), citing Scales (1986, p. 1383).

[9] That view is unlikely to be diminished by such undoubtedly stimulating publications, as Hunter *et al* (2010), which stimulated a similar venture in Australia at the University of Queensland Law School (n.d.).

[10] See quotations from Frankfurter J and Lord MacMillan in Wilson (1990, p. 508) and see Frankfurter (1970).

References

Australian Institute of Judicial Administration. (2014) Statistics 2014, AIJA. Available at: http://www.aija.org.au/JudgesMagistrates2014.pdf, accessed April 2, 2014.

Australian Parliament, Parliament of the Commonwealth of Australia. (1994) *Gender Bias in the Judiciary: Report by the Senate Standing Committee on Legal and Constitutional Affairs.*

Cain, P. (1988) Good and bad bias: a comment on feminist theory and judging, *Southern California Law Review*, 61(6), pp. 1945–1956.

Canadian Judicial Council. (1991) *Commentaries on Judicial Conduct.*

Cardozo, B. (1921) *The Nature of the Judicial Process* (New Haven, Yale University Press).

Chief Justice's Taskforce. (1994, June) *Report of the Chief Justice's Taskforce on Gender Bias.*

Cooney, S. (1993) Gender and judicial selection: should there be more women on the courts? *Melbourne University Law Review*, 19(1), pp. 20–44.

Darbyshire, P. (2011) *Sitting in Judgment – The Working Lives of Judges* (Oxford, Hart Publishing).

Dixon, R. (2010) Female justices, feminism, and the politics of judicial appointment: a re-examination, *Yale Journal of Law and Feminism*, 21(2), pp. 297–338.

Elias, S. (2012) Justice for one half of the human race? Responding to Mary Wollstonecraft's challenge, *The Judicial Review*, 10(4), pp. 399–417.

Frankfurter, F. (1970) The Appointment of a justice, in: P. Kurland (Ed) *Felix Frankfurter on the Supreme Court: Extrajudicial Essays on the Court and the Constitution* (Cambridge, Oxford University Press), pp. 211–217.

Gilligan, C. (1982) *In a Different Voice: Psychological Theory and Women's Development* (Cambridge, Harvard University Press).

Graycar, R. & Morgan, J. (2002) *The Hidden Gender of Law*, 2nd Ed (Annandale, Federation Press).

Hunter, R., McGlynn, C. & Rackley, R. (Eds) (2010) *Feminist Judgments – From Theory to Practice* (Oxford, Hart Publishing).

Judicial Commission of New South Wales. (2006) Bench Book, "Equality Before the Law".

Mack, K. & Roach Anleu, R. (2013) Skills for judicial work: comparing women judges and women magistrates, in: U. Schultz & G. Shaw (Eds) *Gender and Judging* (Oxford, Hart Publishing), pp. 211–232.

Mahoney, K. (1993) Gender bias in judicial decisions, *The Judicial Review*, 1, pp. 197–216.

Malcolm, D. (1993) Gender bias in the administration of justice, *The Judicial Review*, 1, pp. 191–195.

McColl, R. (2014) Celebrating women in the judiciary 2014, Address to *New South Wales Women Lawyers*, Sydney, 27 February. Available at: http://www.supremecourt.lawlink.nsw.gov.au/agdbasev7wr/_assets/supremecourt/m6700011771022/mccoll_270214.pdf, accessed April 2, 2014.

Minamino, K. (2013) Gender and judicial education in Japan, in: U. Schultz & G. Shaw (Eds) *Gender and Judging* (Oxford, Hart Publishing).

National Judicial College of Australia. (2010) *A National Standard for Professional Development for Australian Judicial Officers*. Available at: http://njca.com.au/wp-content/uploads/2013/01/Review-of-the-National-Standard-for-Professional-Development-for-Australian-Judicial-Officer-Report-2010.pdf, accessed April 20, 2014.

Rackley, E. (2013) The Neuberger experiment, *New Law Journal*, 163(7573), pp. 13–14.

Scales, A.C. (1986) The emergence of feminist jurisprudence: an essay, *Yale Law Journal*, 95, pp. 1373–1404.

Schultz, U. & Shaw, G. (2013) Introduction: gender and judging: overview and synthesis, in: U. Schultz & G. Shaw (Eds) *Gender and Judging* (Oxford, Hart Publishing), pp. 3–47.

Scrutton, L.J. (1921) The work of the commercial courts, *Cambridge Law Journal*, 1, pp. 6–20.

University of Queensland Law School. (n.d.) Available at: http://www.law.uq.edu.au/the-australian-feminist-judgments-project, accessed April 7, 2014.

Wilson, B. (1990) Will women judges really make a difference? *Osgoode Hall Law Journal*, 28, pp. 507–522.

Cases

Liteky v. United States 114 S. Ct 1147 (1994).
R v. S (RD) [1997] 3 S.C.R. 484.
Sun v. Minister for Immigration and Ethnic Affairs (1997) 81 F.C.R. 71.

Legislation

Australian Constitution.
Constitution Act 1902 (NSW).
Constitution Act 1934 (SA).
Constitution Act 1975 (Vic).
Constitution of Queensland 2001 (Qld).
County Court Act 1958 (Vic).
District Court Act 1991 (SA).
District Court of Queensland Act 1967 (Qld).
District Court of Western Australia Act 1969 (WA).
Federal Circuit Court of Australia Act 1999 (Cth).
Judges' Retirement Act 1937 (WA).
Judicial Commissions Act 1994 (ACT).
Judicial Officers Act 1986 (NSW).
Magistrates Act 1979 (NT).
Magistrates Act 1983 (SA).
Magistrates Act 1991 (Qld).
Magistrates Court Act 1930 (ACT).
Magistrates Court Act 1987 (Tas).
Magistrates Court Act 2004 (WA).
Magistrates' Court Act 1989 (Vic).
Supreme Court (Judges' Independence) Act 1857 (Tas).
Supreme Court Act 1887 (Tas).
Supreme Court Act 1935 (SA).
Supreme Court Act 1935 (WA).
Supreme Court Act 1979 (NT).
Supreme Court Act 1993 (ACT).
Supreme Court of Queensland Act 1991 (Qld).

Without fear or favour, affection or ill will: addressing gender bias in NSW judicial education

Kate Lumley
Education Division, Judicial Commission of New South Wales, Sydney, Australia

ABSTRACT *This article traces how gender equality has evolved conceptually and provides an overview of the educational initiatives in place for raising gender awareness among members of the NSW judiciary. The author gives examples of gender bias and explores some of the seminal policy and legislative responses at state and federal levels during the reformist decades of the 1970s to the 1990s. North American jurisdictions played an important role in raising judicial awareness of gender bias in the 1980s, with this issue coming to prominence in Australia in the 1990s. The author describes the work of the Judicial Commission of NSW in this area, including training sessions on gender equality, both discrete and as part of integrated education initiatives; its involvement with the National Judicial Orientation Program; and the launch of its* Equality before the Law *Bench Book in 2006.*

Equality is an evolving and controversial ideal (Abella, 1987, p. 4). Since antiquity, concepts of equality have informed Western thought about justice, politics, social structure, ethics, morality and religion. Equality emerged as a modern concept from Enlightenment philosophy and was one-third of the slogan of the French revolutionaries who violently sought freedom from the oppression of the ançien regime. Enlightenment ideas of moral equality were eventually adopted in modern constitutions and declarations of human rights (Stefan & Zalta, 2011).

Defining gender equality

Calls for gender equality found public expression during this era of political and social upheaval. In France, Olympe de Gouges published her *Declaration of the Rights of*

Woman and the Female Citizen in 1791. In Britain the following year, Mary Wollstonecraft published her arguments for substantive equality and a rational education for women (Wollstonecraft, 1792).

While equality has remained the aspirational objective of freedom from oppression and discrimination, the scope of equality has evolved over time. What was regarded as gender equality by Mary Wollstonecraft and Olympe de Gouges, or by the suffragettes in the nineteenth century, or by the second wave of feminism 50 years ago that broadened the debate about women's human rights, has changed with community values. Legal recognition of gay marriage is a contemporary example of the evolving scope of equality. The Australian polity is only beginning the debate about this. The High Court recently struck down the first Australian legislation attempting to give legal recognition to same sex marriage.[1] The court found that legislating for same sex marriage is a matter for the federal parliament and not the Legislative Assembly for the Australian Capital Territory.[2]

Gender inequality has a diversity of meaning both as to its impact and how society should counter it. It embraces the unequal treatment of men and women (that is, discrimination), inequality of opportunity and inequality of outcome. Discrimination arises out of both the "unequal treatment of equals, and, conversely ... the equal treatment of unequals".[3] This expresses the Aristotelian idea of formal equality and underlies the basis of direct and indirect discrimination. Gender bias, a corollary of unequal treatment, has been defined as a "form of subtle but potent discrimination" (Mahoney, 1993, p. 200) and as systemic in nature (ALRC, 1993, DP 54 at [3.41]). Gender bias takes many forms. It manifests in both individual actions and attitudes, in cultural traditions, in institutional and corporate practices, and in the language of the elite. For example, the original *Anti-Discrimination Act*, enacted in NSW in 1977, did not use gender neutral language, instead employing the masculine third person pronoun. It was unlawful for an employer to discriminate against a person "on the ground of *his* sex" (emphasis added).[4] The Act was only changed to gender neutral language 17 years later in 1994.[5]

Gender bias includes undervaluing or not valuing domestic contributions;[6] lack of equal opportunity in the workforce; lack of diversity in senior roles including judicial appointments (McColl, 2006, 2014, pp. 8–10); inequities in pay scales (Glazebrook, 2013, pp. 3–5); reliance on stereotypical attitudes about women and their roles, capacity and ability; the privileging of a male-defined norm, for example, the reasonable man test used in the common law;[7] the disproportionate numbers of female victims of domestic violence and sexual assault (Grech & Burgess, 2011, p. 6; ABS, 2013); the significant underreporting of domestic violence, sexual assault and sexual abuse (Birdsey & Snowball, 2013);[8] and the lack of procedures, until relatively recently, to minimise the trauma for victims in sexual assault trials.[9]

Closing the door on moral conservatism: Australian government reform 1970s–1990s

The Australian federal government began to address the issue of equality for women in the reformist decade of the 1970s. This was the era of social liberalism when

Australia turned its back on the moral conservatism of the Menzies era (Thornton & Luker, 2010, p. 25). No-fault divorce was introduced[10] and free tertiary education. As has been observed, the 1970s saw the development of a "robust civil society [that] enabled feminism in its many guises to emerge and establish itself as a political force for change" (Thornton & Luker, 2010, p. 27). In NSW, the state government enacted the *Anti-Discrimination Act* in 1977. This included Parts III and IV which proscribed discrimination on the ground of sex and marital status in employment and in the provision of specified goods or services subject to certain exceptions.

The following decade saw the Commonwealth of Australia enacting the *Sex Discrimination Act* (SDA) in 1984 and the *Affirmative Action (Equal Opportunity for Women) Act* in 1986. These Acts gave effect to the Commonwealth of Australia's obligations under the Convention on the Elimination of all Forms of Discrimination against Women (CEDAW) which Australia had ratified in 1983.[11]

The early 1990s saw the issue of equality for women firmly on the federal government's policy and legislative agenda (Naylor, 1997). The government funded the National Committee on Violence Against Women which published a highly regarded report in 1992, the *National Strategy on Violence against Women* (Australian Government Publishing Service, 1992). During the election campaign in February 1993, the then Prime Minister announced the federal government's 'New national agenda for women' (Keating, 1993). An element of this agenda was the reference to the Australian Law Reform Commission (ALRC), chaired by the Honourable Elizabeth Evatt AO, to recommend whether legislative or procedural changes should be made to "remove any unjustifiable discriminatory effects of those laws on or of their application to women with a view to ensuring their full equality before the law" (ALRC, 1993, DP 54, p. xi). This culminated in the 1994 two-volume report, *Equality Before the Law: Justice for Women* and *Equality Before the Law: Women's Equality* (ALRC, 1994). In its report, the ALRC reviewed the scope and operation of the SDA and found that the Act fell far short of achieving the substantive objective of equality in law that CEDAW required. The ALRC recommended numerous amendments to the SDA as well as a constitutional guarantee of equality (ALRC, 1994, Report 69, Pt II, Recommendation 4.2).[12] The latter has not occurred. The ALRC report concluded that:

> Despite apparent and real gains over the last decade women still experience discrimination. Gender bias is embedded in the legal system. Addressing specific issues in particular areas will not solve the problem unless that underlying bias is also addressed. (ALRC, 1994, Report 69, Pt I at [1.12])

The need to address gender bias in judicial education

It is axiomatic that the law is administered fairly. Judicial officers in NSW take an oath to administer the law without fear or favour, affection or ill will.[13] The word 'equality' is not specified in the judicial oath but it underpins the oath conceptually. Equal justice is an aspect of the rule of law.[14] Equal justice requires that like cases be treated alike, but where there are relevant differences, allowance should be made for them.[15] This expression is derived from the Aristotelian principle of formal equality, namely, that "things that are alike should be treated alike, while things that are unalike should be treated unalike in proportion to their unalikeness".[16] Equality before the law has come to be recognised as meaning that access to, and the delivery of justice, "requires understanding of and sensitivity to the special requirements and disabilities of particular sections of the community" (Spigelman, 2006). The law has to address both direct and indirect discrimination. To render justice equally, the law must deal with direct discrimination and take account of difference. Indigenous people, ethnic and religious minorities, people with physical and mental disabilities, vulnerable people including children, women, lesbians, gay men, bisexuals, sex and gender diverse people have come to be recognised as having special requirements in the justice system.[17]

Those entrusted to administer the law fairly are informed by their inherited and learned values, cultural assumptions, and ideologies. Although judicial neutrality is a central tenet of the rule of law, it is acknowledged that judicial officers are not ideologically or value neutral. Unconscious judicial bias, built on cultural values and gender and class assumptions, influences the judicial decision-making process (ALRC, 1994, Report 69, Pt II at [2.4]; Mason, 2003, p. 27). As North J put it:

> Decisions made upon assumptions or prejudgments concerning race or gender have been made by many well-meaning judges, unaware of the assumptions or preconceptions which, in fact, governed their decision-making. Thus, actual bias may exist even if the decision-maker did not intend or did not know of their prejudice, or even where the decision-maker believes and says, that they have not prejudged a case.[18]

Public expectations have shifted in the human rights' dominated post-war era to require justification for the exercise of power (Elias, 2012, p. 403). The exercise of judicial authority requires justification. In their decision-making, judicial officers need to be aware of the values of their society so that they can convincingly identify what is in the public interest, and what is 'reasonable' and 'fair'; in other words, the core values of their society (Gleeson, 2007, pp. 329–341; Elias, 2012, p. 405).

Feminist legal scholarship began to deconstruct legal discourse in the 1980s, questioning the claim of law to be rational, objective and neutral (ALRC, 1994, Report 69, Pt II, at [8.17]; Graycar & Morgan, 2002, Ch. 1). It was only a matter of time before the issue of gender bias found its way onto the judicial agenda. North America led the way in raising judicial awareness in the common law world with the work of the National Association of Women Judges' National Task Force on Gender Bias in the Courts. From 1982, State Chief Justices across the United States appointed task forces to investigate gender bias in their courts and recommend reform to legislation, judicial education and the administration of justice. The first task force was appointed in New Jersey in 1982 and by the end of the 1980s, five American states were engaged in implementing the recommendations of their respective task forces and developing sessions in judicial education programmes to address gender bias with a focus on the role of attitudes and values in judicial decision-making (Schafran, 1989, p. 1; Maples & Zimmerman, 1991). In Canada, in 1986, a national judicial conference on equality[19] led to the publication in 1987 of Professor Kathleen Mahoney[20] and Sheilah Martin's book, *Equality and Judicial Neutrality* (Mahoney & Martin, 1987). The Western Judicial Education Centre, a project of the Canadian Association of Provincial Court Judges, developed programmes on gender, race and class bias issues in Canadian judicial training programmes using a variety of adult learning techniques (Parker, 1993, p. 189).

The first-recorded mention of the need to address gender bias in the administration of justice in Australia was on 14 August 1992 when the Supreme Court of Western Australia convened a seminar on this subject (Malcolm, 1993, p. 191). The guest speaker, Professor Mahoney, spoke of the Canadian experience and the Chief Justice of Western Australia, the Honourable Justice Malcolm AC, suggested that Australia had much to learn from the Canadian experience in educating judicial officers about the need to eliminate bias (Malcolm, 1993, p. 195). Professor Mahoney proved to be a trailblazer in raising judicial awareness of gender issues, returning in June 1993 on a visit organised by the National Institute for Law, Ethics and Public Affairs (based at Griffith University, Queensland) to conduct workshops and lectures on gender, race and class bias in the administration of justice in most Australian states (Parker, 1993, p. 189). During this visit, Professor Mahoney spoke at an inter-curial seminar in Sydney convened by the Judicial Commission of NSW (Judicial Commission of NSW, 1992–1993).

Professor Mahoney's 1993 visit coincided with considerable and intense media scrutiny of the Australian judiciary due to a series of gender-biased comments that judges had made during criminal proceedings (Thornton, 2004, p. 4). The most notorious remarks were those of a South Australian Supreme Court judge, Justice Bollen, who during a marital rape trial commented that "rougher than usual handling" was acceptable when a husband was endeavouring to persuade his wife to engage in sexual intercourse (Senate Committee Report, Commonwealth Parliament, Senate Standing Committee on Legal and Constitutional Affairs, 1994, p. 3). The then Prime Minister of Australia, the Honourable Paul Keating, publicly denounced the comments, stating that he was "shocked to read that a judge ... had explicitly condoned the use of violence by a man against his wife" (Keating, 1993, p. 7). A Victorian Supreme Court judge, who in passing sentence on a man who had pleaded guilty to one count of the aggravated rape and one count of the attempted murder of a 17-year-old schoolgirl, said a sentence significantly less than the maximum for the rape offence was warranted as the girl "was not traumatised by the event, indeed was probably comatose at the time" (Senate Committee Report, Commonwealth Parliament, Senate Standing Committee on Legal and Constitutional Affairs, 1994, p. 6). A Commonwealth Parliament Senate Standing Committee on Legal and Constitutional Affairs was briefed to consider whether the

> ... recent publicity surrounding judicial comment in sexual offence cases is a proper reflection of a failure to understand gender issues by the judiciary ... and the appropriate response to any such failure. (p. ix)

The Committee's conclusion was that overt prejudice on the part of the judiciary was not a general problem, but it was "wider than a handful of isolated instances" (Senate

Committee Report, Commonwealth Parliament, Senate Standing Committee on Legal and Constitutional Affairs, 1994, p. xiv). The Committee however stated that systemic gender bias had to be addressed as a "real, significant but largely unconscious, problem" (p. xiv) in the legal system, in legislation and case law, and in the use of "antiquated and inappropriate gender myths and stereotypes when judges sum-up to juries" (p. xiv). The Committee recommended changes to the process of judicial selection and various initiatives in judicial and legal professional education (Ch. 5; Naylor, 1997, p. 432). The process for judicial appointments to federal courts was only revised in 2008 to ensure both greater transparency and merit-based appointments (Roth, 2012). With the change of federal government in 2013, it appears that there are no longer any current judicial appointment processes for any of the federal courts, noted as a "worrying sign" (McColl, 2014, p. 8).[21]

The 1993 Senate Select Committee also recommended that the national Australian (now Australasian) Institute of Judicial Administration (the AIJA) be adequately funded to develop gender awareness programmes in consultation with the courts (Senate Committee Report, Commonwealth Parliament, Senate Standing Committee on Legal and Constitutional Affairs, 1994, Recommendation 5, p. 117). The AIJA had previously accepted federal government grants to develop a national programme on "gender equality and the law" (AIJA, 1993, p. 5). In September 1993, the AIJA sent a number of Australian judges to Vancouver, Canada to attend a faculty training workshop on gender equality. These delegates then advised the AIJA's Gender Equality Committee on strategies to develop suitable programmes in Australia (AIJA, 1994, p. 9). The Judicial Commission of NSW was also represented at the Canadian workshop.[22] Throughout the 1990s, various courts developed their own courses on gender awareness training for judges and staff (ALRC, 1994, [8.66]; Graycar, 1994).

The Australian Law Reform Commission acknowledged in its *Equality before the Law* reference the "considerable activity in the area of gender awareness programmes for the judiciary" since 1993 (ALRC, 1994, Report 69, Pt II [8.68]).[23] For example, the Federal Court of Australia appointed a standing committee to advise the Chief Justice and other judges about gender issues within the court's administration in the provision of its services ([8.66]).[24] The Western Australian Supreme Court established a gender bias task force to develop a judicial education programme ([8.66]). The ALRC made no recommendations in its 1994 report about gender awareness in judicial education, but observed that there was a need "to ensure that the programs are co-ordinated and adequately funded" ([8.68]).

The work of the Judicial Commission of NSW in raising judicial awareness of gender issues will now be examined.

Addressing gender bias in the Judicial Commission judicial education programme

When the Judicial Commission was established in 1987,[25] there were 222 judicial officers in NSW and only 4.5 per cent of judicial officers were women. In 2013, there were 323 permanent judicial officers in NSW and 34.8 per cent of these were women.[26]

This is equivalent to national figures where 8.8 per cent of the judiciary in 1995 were women, rising to 33.5 per cent in 2013 (Australian Women Lawyers, 2013). Although women today are graduating from law school in higher numbers than men and more women are admitted as solicitors than men (Law Council of Australia, 2014, p. 9), women remain underrepresented in the judiciary and among the ranks of partners in law firms and senior counsel.[27]

The Commission's statutory charter is to assist the courts to achieve consistency in sentencing; to organise and supervise an appropriate scheme for the continuing education and training of judicial officers; to investigate complaints concerning the ability or behaviour of a judicial officer; and to give advice to the Minister as the Commission thinks appropriate.[28]

An early objection to the establishment of the Commission and the provision of a judicial education programme was that it would interfere with judicial independence and represent an attack on the separation of powers in NSW (Lumley, 2008, pp. 1–2). These objections were answered when the *Judicial Officers* Act 1986 was amended to establish the Commission as a body independent of the executive arm of government with judicial participation in the education programme being voluntary and judge-led (Lumley, 2008, p. 2). This aligned with the educational philosophy of the Canadian Western Judicial Education Centre which has peer-leadership and judicial independence as key elements. As Professor Mahoney observed, an internal voluntary reform movement will always be more effective than an imposed one (Mahoney, 1993, p. 216; Gleeson, 1998).

The Commission's judicial education policy is not to interfere with judicial discretion but to develop judicial skills, attitudes and knowledge, enhance professional expertise and promote the pursuit of juristic excellence.[29] The overarching purpose of judicial education is to improve the quality of justice so as to maintain public confidence in the impartial and independent administration of justice (Allsop, 2012, p. 440).

The Commission aims to offer up to five judicial education days a year for each judicial officer in NSW in keeping with the national standard developed by the National Judicial College of Australia (NJCA, 2006). The Commission's judicial education programme is multi-faceted, comprising conferences, seminars, field trips, interactive educational sessions, an Aboriginal cultural awareness programme, a 360 degree feedback programme for judicial officers, a voluntary mutual observation programme for magistrates, publications, computer training, and online and printed resources. The programme is based on sound adult education design principles with a focus on experiential and interactive learning, that is, learning based on experience and enhancing judicial skills. The Commission has been influenced by the work of David Kolb and the National Judicial Institute of Canada (Kolb, 1984; Dawson, 2008, p. 47).

Since its inception, the content of the programme has been developed by the education committees of each court in NSW in accordance with the objective of judge-led judicial education. The committees regularly meet to discuss the proposed judicial education programmes for their particular courts. The Judicial Commission's Education Director attends all education committee meetings and provides educational input and support. A Standing Advisory Committee on Judicial Education (SAC) was also established with a representative from each of the court's education committees. The

SAC provides general guidelines and informs each jurisdiction of the activities in the various courts. Information gathered from complaints lodged to the Commission about judicial officers is also used to develop specific education sessions on subjects that include domestic violence, sexual assault issues and cultural awareness.

From 1993, the Commission has offered specific structured sessions relating to gender equality, Aborigines and the law, and ethnicity in the courtroom. The Commission gave evidence to the 1993 Senate Standing Committee on Legal and Constitutional Affairs which specifically noted the provision of education to magistrates about domestic violence (Senate Committee Report, Commonwealth Parliament, Senate Standing Committee on Legal and Constitutional Affairs, 1994, at [5.112]). In evidence given to this inquiry, the Legal Aid Commission of NSW advised that, as a result of this education, there was "an improvement in the attitudes of magistrates in providing access to Apprehended Violence Orders, and action when an order has been breached" (at [5.112]). In 1994, the Judicial Commission gave evidence to the ALRC inquiry that it was providing magistrates with education on domestic violence and on women and the law as part of its education programme (ALRC, 1994, Report 69, Pt II at [8.64]).

Throughout the last two decades, the Commission has continued to offer judicial training on gender equality with the objective of promoting equality before the law in a pluralistic society (Armytage, 1993, 1994). Until 2003, discrete sessions on gender issues, including domestic violence and cultural issues, were offered at the courts' annual conferences, seminars, orientation programmes for magistrates and workshops.[30] Since the 2002–2003 reporting year, the approach has been to integrate gender awareness with a range of issues relating to equality and diversity including Aboriginality, ethnicity and disability.[31] The Commission has developed materials, workshops, seminars and sessions in court conferences to provide information and promote awareness of problems and solutions; to develop practical judicial skills (for example, in courtroom communication, assessment of credit, decision-making and sentencing); and to promote analysis and critical self-reflection of disposition, attitudes and values. Faculty and presenters are drawn from the judiciary, academics, legal practitioners, law reformers, criminologists and professional educators. The Commission evaluates every education session offered to judicial officers to ensure that each session meets its learning objectives, and to review and continually improve the judicial education programme. The low number of complaints made to the Commission each year about judicial ability or behaviour demonstrably attests to the value of the education programme with its objective to enhance judicial capacity and performance and improve the quality of justice (Judicial Commission of NSW, 2012–2013, pp 35–37).[32]

Judicial orientation programmes

Since 1993, the Judicial Commission of NSW has worked jointly with the AIJA (and from 2002 with the NJCA) to offer training in gender bias as part of the National Judicial Orientation Program (NJOP). The NJOP is offered to newly-appointed judicial officers from around Australia on a voluntary basis. The average attendance for each course is about 25 judicial officers. The inaugural programme was held in

October 1994 and, since then, 23 programmes have been offered once or twice a year, depending on demand.[33]

Until 2003, discrete sessions on gender awareness were offered. A rigorous evaluation process led the NJOP Steering Committee to incorporate gender awareness issues into sessions on topics specifically concerned with the art and craft of judging, such as sentencing. Sessions that focus on equality include: "Unconscious judicial prejudice" and "Cultural barriers in the courtroom".

Since 1988, the Judicial Commission has also offered a five-day orientation programme primarily for new magistrates from NSW, although some interstate and Asia Pacific magistrates attend. Participants have consistently rated their approval of this programme at 97 per cent or above.[34] The programme is practical and includes a session with a hypothetical situation requiring participants to reflect on the attitudes and values that they bring to the judicial process with the aim of deconstructing the "myth of impartiality" (Heilpern, 2013).

Equality before the Law Bench Book

In 2005, the Chief Justice of NSW and President of the Judicial Commission, the Honourable JJ Spigelman AC, requested that the Commission develop and publish a Bench Book for judicial officers that would provide the necessary materials and information to assist judicial understanding and sensitivity to the special requirements and disabilities of particular sections of the community (Spigelman, 2006, p. iii). In other words, to assist judicial officers to treat "unequals" with the special measures they require during court proceedings and their interactions with the justice system. Chief Justice Spigelman wished to consolidate the considerable body of material that the Commission had acquired over two decades of operations about equality issues and integrate and transform that material into a loose-leaf service, available in hard copy and soft copy through the Judicial Information Research System (JIRS) and the Commission's public website.[35] The Commission also wished to align with other Australian and international jurisdictions which had similar publications addressing equality issues (Fryer-Smith, 2002; Judicial Studies Board, 2005; Supreme Court of Queensland, 2005). The then Attorney General of NSW, the Honourable John Hatzistergos, launched the *Equality before the Law Bench Book* on 21 June 2006 at the Banco Court, Supreme Court of NSW.

The *Equality before the Law Bench Book* provides practical guidance to assist the judiciary to take into account the special requirements of nine different groups of people who face potential barriers in relation to full and equitable participation in court proceedings. The nine groups are: Aboriginal people; people from culturally and linguistically diverse backgrounds; people with a particular religious affiliation; people with disabilities; children and young people; women; lesbians, gay men and bisexuals; sex and gender diverse people; and self-represented parties.

The Bench Book includes a range of suggested ways for judicial officers to adapt court proceedings to ensure that individuals receive a fair and just outcome. For example:

- employing a different method of communication for those who need it, such as children, people with no or poor English, or people with a communication disability;

- using a different form of oath for people who practise a non-Christian religion;
- knowing and using appropriate terminology so as to avoid causing offence, such as the correct mode of address for people from different ethnic groups or ensuring that religious leaders are addressed by the appropriate title;
- adjusting timing and length of court appearances to take account of people with a particular disability or people with childcare responsibilities;
- using a translator or interpreter when a witness's English is not good enough to cope with the demands of the courtroom;
- intervening in cross-examination to disallow unfair or inappropriate questions;
- ensuring that the cultural customs or values of a particular person are respected by everyone in the court.

Chapter 7 of the Bench Book focuses on women, providing current statistics about women in NSW; information about gender bias with examples of how this can arise and how to avoid it; practical considerations for judicial officers regarding modes of addressing women, use of language and terminology; timing of proceedings, breaks and adjournments; information about domestic violence and sexual assault matters (including common myths and assumptions); and how women may be particularly affected by sentencing decisions (for example the impact of a mother's incarceration on a family), personal injury compensation and property division in family law disputes.

In 2006, the *Equality before the Law Bench Book* received the AIJA's Award for Excellence in Judicial Administration, a biennial award made in recognition of a significant contribution to the furtherance of judicial administration in Australia.

Conclusion

Two decades after feminist legal scholarship began to question the gender bias inherent in the common law, education about gender equality was introduced to the Australian judicial training agenda in 1993. Taking its cue from developments in North America, the Judicial Commission of NSW committed to raising judicial awareness about conscious and unconscious gender bias through its voluntary judicial education programme, along with several Australian courts and the AIJA. The Commission's focus has been on the practice and procedure of judging – the judicial method – to assist the judicial officers of NSW to administer the law without fear or favour, affection or ill will.

Acknowledgements

The author acknowledges the review and assistance of Ruth Windeler, Education Director, Judicial Commission of NSW, and Maree D'Arcy, Librarian, Judicial Commission of NSW.

Disclosure statement

No potential conflict of interest was reported by the author.

Notes

[1] In *Cth v ACT* (2013) 88 ALJR 118, the High Court struck down the *Marriage Equality (Same Sex) Act* 2013 (ACT) as it was found to be wholly inconsistent with the *Marriage Act* 1961 (Cth).

[2] Ibid at [56–58].

[3] *Castlemaine Tooheys Ltd v SA* (1990) 169 CLR 436 at 480.

[4] *Anti-Discrimination Act* 1977, s 25(1).

[5] By the *Anti Discrimination (Amendment) Act* 1994 (commenced on 8 August 1994). The repealed *Interpretation Act* 1897, s 21(a), provided that "Words importing the masculine gender shall include females".

[6] See the High Court's decision in *Daly v Thiering* (2013) 249 CLR 381 (Crennan, Kiefel, Bell, Gageler and Keane JJ in a joint judgment) which reversed the NSW Court of Appeal (NSWCA) decision in *Daly v Thiering* [2013] NSWCA 25. The NSWCA dismissed an appeal from the first instance decision in *Thiering v Daly* (2011) 83 NSWLR 498 where Garling J held that damages claimed in proceedings for the gratuitous attendant care provided by a mother to her son catastrophically injured in a motor vehicle accident could be awarded if a statutory scheme (the Lifetime Care and Support Scheme) had not paid or accepted an obligation to pay for such services for the past. Following the NSWCA decision, the NSW Parliament amended the *Motor Accidents Compensation Act* 1999 (repealing s 130A) to clarify that the Scheme is only obliged to pay for assessed treatment and care needs and is not obliged to pay for treatment and care provided on a gratuitous basis: *Motor Accidents and Lifetime Care and Support Schemes Legislation Amendment Act* 2012, Sch 2 [5] (commenced on 25 June 2012). In effect, the Scheme abolished *Griffiths v Kerkemeyer* ([1977] 139 CLR 161) damages. The High Court held that a participant in the Scheme was prevented from recovering damages for economic loss for their treatment and care needs which were rendered gratuitously: at [36].

[7] As critiqued in the Canadian decision, *R v Lavallee* [1990] 1 SCR 852 at [43], [55].

[8] Birdsey and Snowball (2013) reported that only half (51.8 per cent) of victims report their most recent domestic violence incident to police in NSW.

[9] For example, the *Criminal Procedure Act* 1986 has, since 2000, contained a series of evidentiary and procedural provisions aimed at minimising the trauma of a sexual assault trial for a complainant. These provisions have been further strengthened since 2003.

[10] By the *Family Law Act* 1975 (Cth).

[11] And also to parts of the International Labour Organisation Convention 156, Workers with family responsibilities, 1981 (entry into force generally 11 August 1983; entry into force for Australia 30 March 1991). Australia ratified CEDAW at a special signing ceremony at the UN World Conference for the Decade of Women on 28 July 1983, having signed it in 1980. Available at: https://treaties.un.org/Pages/ViewDetails.aspx?src=TREATY&mtdsg_no=IV-8&chapter=4&lang=en.

[12] Constitutional entrenchment was recommended as "a long-term goal".

[13] *Oaths Act* 1900 (NSW), Sch 4.

[14] *Green v The Queen* (2011) 244 CLR 462 at [28].

[15] *Lowe v The Queen* (1984) 154 CLR 606 at 617–618; *Postiglione v The Queen* (197) 189 CLR 295 at 301; *Wong v The Queen* (2001) 207 CLR 584 at [65]; *Jimmy v R* (2010) 77 NSWLR 540 at [255].

[16] *Jimmy v R*, Ibid, at [256], citing Aristotle (1925).

[17] These categories are recognised in the Judicial Commission of NSW (2006), *Equality before the Law Bench Book*.

[18] *Sun v Minister for Immigration and Ethnic Affairs* (1997) 81 FCR 71 at 135.

[19] The Socialisation of Judges to Equality Issues Conference, The University of Calgary, Faculty of Law, Banff, Alberta, May 1986, referred to in Mahoney (1993) at p. 199.

[20] Professor of Law at the University of Calgary, Canada, and a former director of the UN-sponsored International Project to Promote Fairness in Judicial Processes.

[21] See also <www.ag.gov.au/LegalSystem/Courts/Pages/Courtappointments.aspx>.

[22] By the Chair of the Standing Advisory Committee on Judicial Education.

[23] See also [8.63] – [8.66].

[24] This became the 'Equality and the Law' committee the following decade: Federal Court of Australia, *Annual Report 2006–2007*, p. 36.
[25] By the *Judicial Officers Act* 1986.
[26] Judicial Commission of NSW, unpublished data, 16 December 2013.
[27] As at 30 June 2013, 9.7 per cent of senior counsel were women whereas 20 per cent of barristers are women: NSW Bar Association, *Annual Report 2012–13*, p. 11. The *National Attrition and Re-engagement (NARs) Study*, (2014), reports that men are twice as likely as women to be a partner in private practice. The national study surveyed 3,801 practising lawyers, or close to 1 in 10 members of the legal profession in Australia (Ibid, p. 4).
[28] *Judicial Officers Act* 1986, ss 8, 9, 11, Pt 6.
[29] Judicial Commission of NSW, *Continuing Judicial Education Policy*, reproduced in the annual reports of the Judicial Commission at Appendix 3.
[30] As recorded in the Judicial Commission of NSW's annual reports from 1993 to 2003.
[31] The Judicial Commission of NSW's *Annual Report 2002–03* lists "social awareness issues, including migrants, interpreters, ethnicity and gender" as an education topic in Appendix 4, p. 57.
[32] For example, in the 2012–13 reporting year, the Commission received 71 complaints about 53 judicial officers. There were 350 (permanent and acting) judicial officers in NSW in 2012–13. Of these 71 complaints, 13 complaints alleged bias on the part of the judicial officer. See Judicial Commission of NSW, *Annual Report 2012–2013*, pp. 35–37.
[33] Judicial Commission unpublished data, 13 December 2013.
[34] These results are reported in the education section of the Judicial Commission of NSW's annual reports since 2007 in figures showing the satisfaction ratings for the Commission's education programmes over a five-year period.
[35] Available at: http://www.judcom.nsw.gov.au.

References

Abella, R. (1987) The dynamic nature of equality, in: K.E. Mahoney & S.L. Martin (Eds) *Equality and Judicial Neutrality* (Toronto, Carswell), pp. 3–9.

Allsop, J. (2012) Continuing judicial education: the Australian experience, *The Judicial Review*, 10(4), pp. 439–454.

Aristotle, Ross W.D. (Trans) (1925) *Ethica Nichomacea, Book V3* (Oxford, Clarendon Press), at 1131a-6.

Armytage, L. (1993) Continuing judicial education: the education programme of the Judicial Commission of NSW, *Journal of Judicial Administration*, 3(1), pp. 28–46.

Armytage, L. (1994) Judicial education on gender equality: the educational response, submission to the ALRC Equality before the Law Inquiry.

Australian Bureau of Statistics (ABS). (2013) *Recorded Crime – Victims*, ABS cat no 4501.0, Canberra, Available at: www.abs.gov.au/ausstats/abs@.nsf/Lookup/by%20Subject/4510.0~2013~Main%20Features~Sexual%20Assault~9.

Australian Government Publishing Service. (1993) *New National Agenda for Women* (Canberra).

Australian (now Australasian) Institute of Judicial Administration (AIJA). (1993) *Annual Report for the Year Ended June 1993* (Melbourne) p. 5.

Australian (now Australasian) Institute of Judicial Administration (AIJA). (1994) *Annual Report for the Year Ended June 1994*, (Melbourne) p. 9.

Australian Law Reform Commission (ALRC). (1993) *Equality before the Law*, Discussion Paper 54, (Sydney) (ALRC DP 54).

Australian Law Reform Commission (ALRC). (1994) *Equality before the Law*, Report 69, (Sydney). The report is divided into two parts: Pt 1, *Equality before the law: justice for women*, (ALRC Report 69: Pt I), and Pt II, *Equality before the law: women's equality*, (ALRC Report 69: Pt II).

Australian Women Lawyers. (2013) *Gender in the Australian Judiciary 2013 v 1995*, media release, Adelaide.

Birdsey, E. & Snowball, L. (2013) Reporting violence to police: a survey of victims attending domestic violence services, *Issues Paper No 91*, BOCSAR, Sydney.

Commonwealth Parliament, Senate Standing Committee on Legal and Constitutional Affairs. (1994) *Gender bias and the judiciary*, (Senate Committee Report), Canberra.

Dawson, T.B. (2008) Lessons learned for experiential, skills-based judicial education, *Judicial Officer's Bulletin*, 20(6), pp. 47–49.

de Gouges, O. (1791) Declaration of the rights of woman and the female citizen. Available at: http://www.academia.edu/3100911/Olympe_de_Gouges._1791._Declaration_of_the_Rights_of_Woman_and_of_the_Woman-Citizen.

Elias, S. (2012) Justice for one half of the human race? Responding to Mary Wollstonecraft's challenge, *The Judicial Review*, 10(4), pp. 399–417 at 403.

Fryer-Smith, S. (2002) *Aboriginal Benchbook for Western Australian Courts* (Victoria, AIJA Model Indigenous Benchbook Project). Available at: www.aija.org.au/online/ICABenchbook/Intro.pdf.

Glazebrook, S. (2013) It is just a matter of time and other myths, revised version of a paper presented at the *Get Up and Speak 2013 seminar*, Wellington, New Zealand. Available at: www.courtsofnz.govt.nz/speechpapers.

Gleeson, A.M. (1998) Performing the role of the judge, *Judicial Officer's Bulletin*, 10(8), pp. 57–60.

Gleeson, A.M. (2007) A core value, *The Judicial Review*, 8(3), pp. 329–341.

Graycar, R. (1994) Gendered assumptions in family law, Paper presented at the *Gender Awareness Seminar, Family Court of Australia*, Kooralbyn, Queensland.

Graycar, R. & Morgan, J. (2002) *The Hidden Gender of Law* (Sydney, Federation Press, 2nd edn).

Grech, K. & Burgess, M. (2011) *Trends and Patterns in Domestic Violence Assaults: 2001–2010*, Issue Paper No 61, NSW Bureau of Crime Statistics and Research (BOCSAR), Sydney. Available at: www.bocsar.nsw.gov.au/agdbasev7wr/bocsar/documents/pdf/bb61.pdf.

Heilpern, D. (2013) Alligator River bias presentation, presentation to the magistrate's orientation program, unpublished material.

Judicial Commission of NSW. (1992–1993) *Annual Report* (Sydney, Judicial Commission).

Judicial Commission of NSW. (2006) *Equality before the Law Bench Book* (Sydney, Judicial Commission).

Judicial Commission of NSW. (2012–2013) *Annual Report* (Sydney, Judicial Commission), pp. 35–37.

Judicial Studies Board. (2005) *Equal Treatment Bench Book* (London, Judicial Studies Board) (now superseded by the 2013 edition). Available at: www.judiciary.gov.uk/publications-and-reports/judicial-college/Pre+2011/equal-treatment-bench-book.

Law Council of Australia. (2014) *National Attrition and Re-engagement (NARS) Study*, Final Report. Available at: www.lawcouncil.asn.au/lawcouncil/index.php/law-council-media/news/324-nars.

Keating, P.J. (1993) National agenda for women, speech presented at the Bankstown Town Hall. See Office of the Status of Women, Department of Prime Minister and Cabinet, *Women: shaping and sharing the future: the new national agenda for women, 1993–2000*, Australian Government Publishing Service, Canberra.

Kolb, D. (1984) *Experiential Learning: Experience as the Source of Learning and Development* (Englewood Cliffs, New Jersey, Prentice Hall).

Lumley, K. (2008) *From Controversy to Credibility: 20 Years of the Judicial Commission of NSW*, Judicial Commission of NSW. Available at: www.judcom.nsw.gov.au/about-the-commission.

McColl, R. (2006) Women in the law, address to the *Anglo-Australasian Society of Lawyers*, Sydney.

McColl, R. (2014) Celebrating women in the judiciary 2014, address to *Women Lawyers Association of NSW*, Union, University and Schools Club, Sydney. Available at: www.supremecourt.lawlink.nsw.gov.au/agdbasev7wr/_assets/supremecourt/m6700011771022/mccoll_270214.pdf.

Mahoney, K.E. (1993) Gender bias in judicial decisions, *The Judicial Review*, 1(3), pp. 197–216.

Mahoney, K.E. & Martin, S.L. (Eds) (1987) *Equality and Judicial Neutrality* (Toronto, Carswell).

Malcolm, D. (1993) Gender bias in the administration of justice, *The Judicial Review*, 1(3), pp. 191–196.

Maples, M. & Zimmerman, G. (1991) *The Crucial Nature of Values and Attitudes in Judicial Decision-making* (Reno, National Council of Juvenile and Family Court Judges).

Mason, K. (2003) Unconscious judicial prejudice, in: *A Matter of Judgment: Judicial Decision-making and Judgment Writing* (Sydney, Judicial Commission of NSW).

National Judicial College of Australia (prepared by Roper AM, C). (2006) *National Standard for Professional Development for Australian Judicial Officers*. Available at: http://njca.com.au/wp-content/uploads/2013/01/A-National-Standard-for-Professional-Development.pdf.

Naylor, B. (1997) Equality before the law: mission impossible? A review of the Australian Law Reform Commission's Report Equality Before the Law, *Monash University Law Review*, 23(2), pp. 423–440.

Parker, C. (1993) Gender bias: a timely visit, *Alternative Law Journal*, 18(4), pp. 188–190.

Roth, L. (2012) *Judicial appointments*, Briefing paper No 3/2012, NSW Parliamentary Research Library, Sydney.

Schafran, L.H. (1989) *Planning for Evaluation: Guidelines for Task Forces on Gender Bias in the Courts* (Women Judges' Fund for Justice), p. 1. Available at: womenlaw.stanford.edu/pdf/schafran.pdf.

Spigelman, J.J. (2006) Foreword to Judicial Commission of NSW, *Equality before the Law Bench Book*, Sydney. Available at: http://www.judcom.nsw.gov.au/publications/benchbks/equality.

Stefan, G. & Zalta, E.N. (Eds) (2011) Equality, *Stanford Encyclopaedia of Philosophy (Spring 2011 edn)*. Available at: http://plato.stanford.edu/archives/spr2011/entries/equality.

Supreme Court of Queensland. (2005) *Equal Treatment Benchbook* (Brisbane, Supreme Court of Queensland Library). Available at: www.courts.qld.gov.au/information-for-lawyers/benchbooks-and-ucpr-bulletin.

Thornton, M. (2004) The legal profession: gender, legality and authority, address to the *Australian Lawyers and Social Change Conference*, Canberra.

Thornton, M. & Luker, T. (2010) The *Sex Discrimination Act* and its rocky rite of passage, in: M. Thornton (Ed), *Sex Discrimination in Uncertain Times* (Canberra, Australian National University ePress), pp. 25–45.

Wollstonecraft, M. (1792) *A Vindication of the Rights of Woman: With Strictures on Political and Moral Subjects*, 2nd ed (London, J Johnson).

Acts

Affirmative Action (Equal Opportunity for Women) Act (Cth)
Anti-Discrimination Act 1977 (NSW)
Anti-Discrimination (Amendment) Act 1994 (NSW)
Criminal Procedure Act 1986 (NSW)
Family Law Act 1975 (Cth)
Judicial Officers Act 1986 (NSW)
Motor Accidents Compensation Act 1999 (NSW)
Motor Accidents and Lifetime Care and Support Schemes Legislation Amendment Act 2012 (NSW)
Oaths Act 1900 (NSW)
Sex Discrimination Act 1984 (Cth)

Cases

Castlemaine Tooheys Ltd v SA (1990) 169 CLR 436
Cth v ACT (2013) 88 ALJR 118
Daly v Thiering [2013] NSWCA 25
Daly v Thiering (2013) 249 CLR 381
Green v The Queen (2011) 244 CLR 462
Griffiths v Kerkemeyer (1977) 139 CLR 161
Jimmy v R (2010) 77 NSWLR 540
Lowe v The Queen (1984) 154 CLR 606
Postiglione v The Queen (197) 189 CLR 295
R v Lavallee [1990] 1 SCR 852
Sun v Minister for Immigration and Ethnic Affairs (1997) 81 FCR 71
Thiering v Daly (2011) 83 NSWLR 498
Wong v The Queen (2001) 207 CLR 584

Index

Note: Page numbers followed by 'n' refer to notes

For Product Safety Concerns and Information please contact our EU
representative GPSR@taylorandfrancis.com
Taylor & Francis Verlag GmbH, Kaufingerstraße 24, 80331 München, Germany

www.ingramcontent.com/pod-product-compliance
Ingram Content Group UK Ltd.
Pitfield, Milton Keynes, MK11 3LW, UK
UKHW050054200926
475702UK00019B/2838
* 9 7 8 0 3 6 7 0 2 9 7 1 5 *